WOMEN SOLDIERS

Women Soldiers

Images and Realities

Edited by

Elisabetta Addis
Lecturer, University of Rome 'La Sapienza'

Valeria E. Russo
Former Academic Coordinator of the European Culture Research Centre
European University Institute, Florence

and

Lorenza Sebesta
Research Assistant, European University Institute, Florence

Consultant Editor: Jo Campling

St. Martin's Press

Editorial matter and selection © Elisabetta Addis, Valeria E. Russo
and Lorenza Sebesta 1994
Text © The Macmillan Press Ltd 1994
Chapter 5 © Cynthia H. Enloe 1994

First published in Great Britain 1994 by
THE MACMILLAN PRESS LTD
Houndmills, Basingstoke, Hampshire RG21 2XS
and London
Companies and representatives
throughout the world

A catalogue record for this book is available
from the British Library.

ISBN 0-333-60092-4 hardcover
ISBN 0-333-60093-2 paperback

Printed in Great Britain by
Antony Rowe Ltd
Chippenham, Wiltshire

First published in the United States of America 1994 by
Scholarly and Reference Division,
ST. MARTIN'S PRESS, INC.,
175 Fifth Avenue,
New York, N.Y. 10010

ISBN 0-312-12073-7 (cloth)
ISBN 0-312-12074-5 (paper)

Library of Congress Cataloging-in-Publication Data
Women soldiers : images and realities / edited by Elisabetta Addis,
Valeria E. Russo and Lorenza Sebesta.
p.   cm.
Includes bibliographical references and index.
ISBN 0-312-12073-7. — ISBN 0-312-12074-5 (pbk.)
1. United States—Armed Forces—Women.   2. Women soldiers—United
States—Social conditions.   I. Addis, E. (Elisabetta)   II. Russo,
Valeria E.   III. Sebesta, Lorenza.
UB418.W65W68   1994
355'.0082—dc20   93-39270
                                                                    CIP

Contents

PART III   CASE STUDIES

Acknowledgements

We wish to thank the Forum on the Problems of Peace and War, Florence, and the European Culture Research Center at the European University Institute, Florence, for research support, and Elena Brizio and Jan Fraser for translating some of the material into English. Opinions and errors as usual are only our own.

Notes on the Contributors

Elisabetta Addis, born in Italy and trained in the USA, is Lecturer of Economics at the University of Rome. Her last publications on the topic 'Women and the military service' are *The Effects of Military Spending on Women in Italy*, in E. Isaksson (ed.) *Women and the Military System* (London, 1987); 'La spesa militare come redistribuzione di risorse economiche' in L. Menapace and C. Ingrao (eds.) *Nè indifesa nè in divisa* (Rome, 1988). She is vice president of IAFFE and has published work on Italian and European monetary policy.

Cynthia H. Enloe is Professor of Government at Clark University, Worcester, Massachusetts. Her book, *Does Khaki Become You?* (Boston, 1983) is a milestone in the study of military women. Her most recent effort, *Bananas, Beaches and Bases* extends the study to the effect of the military on the life of women outside it (military wives, daughters, prostitutes, defense industry workers).

Maria Graeff-Wassink, specialist in Maghrebin sociology, was Research Assistant at Amsterdam University before leaving the country to live for several years in the Middle East, including Morocco, Lebanon, Syria, Libya and Iran; she spent four years researching her book *La femme en armes. Kedafi feministe?* (Paris, 1990).

Patricia B. Hanna received her Master's degree in Clinical Social Work from Boston College. Since 1988 she has worked as a Clinical Supervisor for the US Navy's drug and alcohol programme, initially in Rota, Spain, and then in Naples, Italy, after moving to Florence in 1990. She received the Navy's 'Preceptor of the Year' Award for Outstanding Performance, in July 1993. Publications include work in the areas of social and economic policy, occupational mental health programmes and women in the military.

Virgilio Ilari is Professor of Military Institutions at the Catholic University of Milan and is the most reputed expert on postwar Italian military history. He has written various books on military subjects and is the author of a five-volume encyclopedia of military service in Italy from Machiavelli to the present day.

Valeria E. Russo, philosopher, UNICEF–ICDC Consultant, was the Academic Coordinator of the European Culture Research Center at the European University Institute in Florence. Her publications include: *Franz Borkenau* (Florence, 1988); *Theodor Lessing, La civiltá maledetta* (coeditor) (Naples, 1984); *Lo specchio infranto, Territori della differenza* (editor) (Florence, 1989); *La questione dell'esperienza* (editor) (Florence, 1991).

Lorenza Sebesta has been working in the field of security studies for over ten years; after completing a PhD thesis on European security problems in the 1950s, she published a book on the same topic, *L'Europa indifesa*, (Florence, 1991); she is currently Research Assistant at the European University Institute in Florence, History Department, working on a project sponsored by the European Space Agency dealing with national space policies.

Julie Wheelwright is the author of *Amazons and Military Maids* (London, 1989) and *The Fatal Lover: Mata Hari and the Myth of Women Espionage* (London, 1992). She acted as a consultant for an Open University course on Women in Science and Technology, producing a radio programme on female soldiers for BBC Radio 5. She has written extensively on issues about women and war for newspapers, magazines and academic journals in the UK and elsewhere.

Introduction
Elisabetta Addis, Valeria E. Russo and Lorenza Sebesta

The essays collected in this book deal with a new situation: the presence of women as soldiers and officers in regular armed forces.

Taken as a whole, the studies are a comprehensive, inter-disciplinary analysis of the consequences of female military service. These consequences are economic, psychological and political. They affect women who enlist, and women who do not wish to enlist in the armed forces, and the collective image of the 'soldier', the 'warrior' and the 'enemy'.

This book shows how both the options presently available to women – perpetuation of exclusion or complete assimilation to the prevailing, masculine military model – have heavy costs for women.

Armed forces open to women are a recent development. The information material supplied by the defence ministries of countries that employ women soldiers frequently refers to an earlier, often mythical, date of origin: they are presented as the heirs of former auxiliary corps or of legendary national Amazon-style warriors. Nonetheless, recruitment under the current policies, and a contingent of a size comparable to the present, date from the early 1970s.

In the armed forces of the USA, which are the most cultur-ally influential because of their strategic importance in the military equilibria of the contemporary world, women make up 11 per cent of personnel in service. The participation of 33,000 American women soldiers in the Gulf War made world public opinion aware of their existence.

Women soldiers are present in countries widely different in culture, ideology, political position and geography, such as Israel and Libya, Brunei and China.

In Italy, the only NATO (North Atlantic Treaty Organiza-tion) country with exclusively male armed forces, the topic is of particular interest because the Defence Ministry has proclaimed the opening of military structures to women to be imminent. This proposal revived, in the general public and especially within the women's movements, a debate in which the arguments in favour of equal rights and opportunities are opposed to arguments in favour of preserving, and possibly extending to men, those values and attitudes that make women different. Such values appear all the more valuable for being traditionally associated with the pursuit of peace.

What then are the consequences of women's entry into the armed forces? The traditional military is commonly regarded as the paradigmatic model of masculine organization. The behavioural codes, activities and objectives of military organization have hitherto assumed masculinity as a basic value. But masculinity, like femininity, is a complex cultural construct whose constituent features change over time. And it is hard to see how and why the military should be regarded as more male than other institutions like universities or the judiciary, likewise created by and for centuries the exclusive preserve of men.

Yet women's participation in the military appears to many to specifically contradict a deeply ingrained image of femininity. By the same token, many fear that the presence of women would undermine the masculinity of the military itself, and that the armed forces would, by opening to women, lose some essential characteristic, held necessary to fulfil their purpose.

Opening to women has many consequences for the armed forces and their image. The military experience was often represented in the past as the crucial experience in which the boy is forged into a man, his masculinity tested and confirmed. The presence of women contributes to the erasure of this symbolic feature, that constitutes one of the residual attractions of military service for young people of the male sex. Within the armed forces, the internal mode of operation, governed by the twin principles of authority and hierarchy, is put to the test when the position of hierarchical authority is occupied by someone traditionally in a subordinate position within the family and in society. From the logistical viewpoint, the armed forces have to learn to cope with the needs of female personnel who lack the organizational and emotional support structure constituted by a wife, or indeed are themselves fulfilling the threefold function of wife, mother and soldier.

Studies by contributors to this book show that women soldiers discover quickly what is meant by the masculinity of the armed forces: brought into this male institution, women encounter particular difficulties that have not hitherto been adequately explored. There has in fact been very little research into the specific experiences of women soldiers, into the reasons for their choice, into the psychological and economic problems and into the problems of organization of their personal life that they have to face. There has been little research, that is, from the woman's viewpoint: before introducing military service, the military hierarchies of the various countries assessed its consequences from their own point of view, centring their analysis not so much on the women as on the armed forces themselves. The presence of women soldiers could potentially create notable difficulties in terms of organization, culture and military ideology. Nonetheless, women are increasingly a highly skilled group within the labour force, and the growing administrative complexity of the military organization and the technological progress in weaponry make high levels of qualification and specialization increasingly necessary, expecially in all-volunteer armed forces. From the viewpoint of an optimal administration of human resources, the armed forces of many countries decided they could not afford to give up a source of educated and inexpensive manpower – or womanpower.

We must remember, moreover, that the move to open armed forces to women has helped to restore legitimacy to the armed forces which in many countries in the 1970s were going through a deep crisis of public consensus. The considerations of these positive aspects of female military service do not change the fact that their presence causes inconvenience and burden, as it involves undesired structural, psychological and organizational adjustments.

Although the entrance of women is consistent with the gains in equality in other sectors and occupations, the admission of women to the military came after pressure from military spheres, not from the women's movements themselves. Women's organized political groups never initiated a request for military service, although they afterwards strongly supported the demands for parity within the armed forces coming from the new female personnel.

This latter fact is somewhat peculiar, because the existence or otherwise of female military service has major consequences for women who are not soldiers, including those who would never wish to enlist. From the viewpoint of gender economic policy, that is, of the distribution of available resources between the two sexes in society, if women are excluded from the armed forces then military expenditure represents a channel through which public expenditure creates exclusively male employment, granting male citizens alone the possibility of income and offering them the possibility of acquiring professional qualifications. Consequently, since female and male labour are not considered perfectly interchangeable by civilian employers, the relative scarcity of young males raises salaries, while the relative abundance of young women makes women's employment and wages relatively lower. Additionally, professional skills acquired during military service are reflected in relatively higher wages for men.

Moreover, when there are no women in the armed forces, the purchasing decisions on a huge mass of final goods, namely military supplies, are left in the hands of members of the male sex alone. Even if the military budget is subject to parliamentary approval, the details of commitments and distribution of orders among various firms is influenced by the leaders of the armed forces. This too contributes to a strengthening of the status of the military hierarchies, from which women are excluded.

The right to defend one's country, in sum, opens access to what has been defined as 'first class citizenship', corresponding to both material privileges and greater political power. This correspondence, self-evident in military dictatorships, is still present in parliamentary democracies too, helping to perpetuate the preponderant presence of individuals of the male sex in the legislative and executive bodies and in other positions of power.

The existence of women soldiers and the image of them filtering through the media has important consequences for the construction of femininity, that is, for the collective image of what a woman is and what it is appropriate for to her to be, and for the image that each woman may have of herself.

In the collective imagination, women are sources of mediation and dialogue, guarantors of domestic tranquillity in a competitive world, bearers of life, rather than of death. Women have for centuries been the depositaries and custodians of the positive values of peace and meekness on behalf of the whole of society. How, then, can this traditional image of femininity coexist with the image emerging in the media since the invasion of Panama and particularly the Gulf War, represented by a woman in uniform wearing fatigues like a man and wielding a gun like a man, ready to kill on command like a soldier, if need be?

The image of the woman soldier coming through the media during the Gulf War was, as Cynthia Enloe remarks in her essay, filtered through the ideology of professionalism. The Gulf War was a peculiar war: the Saudis, fearing the fundamentalists' reactions to the alliance with the USA, imposed strict rules banning alcohol, prostitution, and in general limiting contact between the Allied soldiers and the population. It was a technological war, fought by planes, computers and radars. Blood was not shed in direct, body against body, confrontations. And, for the Allies, i.e. the armed forces which we know about, there were very few casualties.

The soldier of this war was a technician: prowess was a matter of brains, not of brawn. The ideology of professionalism here becomes the key to a reconciliation of the two images, allowing both men and the women to accept the idea that a soldier can be a woman, that a woman can do the job of a soldier. The ideology of professionalism requires that no-one's personal, political, religious and cultural positions – including, in this case, gender – should influence the way that the work is done. If a job is done professionally it does not matter who does it. Professionalism is the yardstick.

This ideology in part neutralizes the masculinity of the military character, helping to place the armed forces within a symbolic universe dominated no longer by the values of force, capacity for command, obedience to orders, and boldness, but by those typical of bureaucratic organizations, such as efficiency, productivity and obedience to formal procedures.

The image of the woman soldier emerging after the Gulf War bears little resemblance to the ancient images of the armed woman. The ancient image derived in part from myth – the Amazon – and in part from actual armed participation by women in people's wars and guerrilla warfare. The Amazon was an awesome figure, her contrast with femininity symbolically underlined by the mythological removal of the left breast to facilitate archery. Women who fought in revolutionary wars testified to the exceptional character of the historical circumstances, and were restored to their civilian status after the fight was over, while their male comrades, in case of victory, became the backbone of the regular armed forces.

The new image of the woman soldier sharply contrasts, too, with the traditional image of the patriotic woman, as affirmed in the first half of this century. The patriotic woman was offered as a model by national propaganda in contemporary wars because it served in various ways the needs of the military. There are different versions of the image of the patriotic woman: she might be a mother prepared to bear sons and sacrifice them to the motherland, or a housewife prepared to follow her military husband in his various shifts of location, maintaining his honour through grace, fidelity, order and other domestic virtues. She could be a supportive sister or faithful fiancée', or an impartial Red Cross nurse. She could be, never openly celebrated but certainly taken into consideration by military hierarchies, a prostitute. The prostitutes were supposed to be the 'necessary' support for the sexual and sentimental life of the troops and hence were always present, tolerated and even encouraged in the vicinity of barracks and the front, patriotic too in their own way. These figures cannot disappear with the appearance of the woman soldier, since the military organization still needs women who fulfil these functions. The mother, the wife, the Red Cross nurse, the prostitute, exemplify the complex, contradictory relationship between women, the military and war. Despite historical exclusion from regular armies, it is incorrect to assert that armed conflict was alien to women, and that women had no part in wars.

A vast and interesting literature exists concerning women and war, stimulated partly by the lively development of women's history in the last decade under the impetus of feminist demands. It has explored the consequences of a war economy on the civilian female workforce, the attitudes and values of the women who live alongside and constitute the support structure for individual soldiers, the birth, in times of war, of specific women's organizations to support the military structure, promoting consensus for the war effort and providing an auxiliary service, the propagandistic use of women in the context of publicity campaigns in favour of military mobilization.

While taking account of the main findings of this literature, our research narrows its focus to women soldiers in the contemporary world, that is, to women directly enrolled in the regular armed forces and trained in the use of weapons for the active participation in armed conflict on terms of (quasi) equality with soldiers of the other sex.

The figure of the patriotic woman in her various manifestations as mother, wife, nurse, etc., subordinated in many respects to military needs, is just as militarized an image of femininity, albeit in a different form, as that of the woman in uniform carrying a rifle. The patriotic woman is also a variant of the positive image of the non-aggressive, meek human being prepared to listen and offer help, capable of daily sacrifice, and thus no less heroic than the male hero fighter. The woman soldier in fatigues who carries a rifle represents, undoubtedly, a woman who has achieved all you can in formal, if not real, equality with men.

Despite the apparent reconciliation brought about by the ideology of professionalism, these two antagonistic images of militarized femininity which we have described coexist in the collective imagination. Their coexistence presents the women's movement with a serious political problem in dealing with the question of female military service.

It is the same problem that often emerges when policies to protect the interests of women are proposed, like maternity leaves or exemption of mothers from night work. When the issue is military service, this difficulty becomes more clear. It is difficult to find innovative solutions to the dichotomy between policies of equality and policies of 'difference', i.e. meant to preserve and extend to men traditionally feminine attitudes and values. Women will remain subordinate until they achieve equal rights and effective equality with men, but not at the cost of becoming like traditional men. Men should change too. Formal equality to a traditionally masculine model constrains women, and makes them feel ill at ease. Women neither can nor want to abandon a difference in attitudes and behaviour. The problem is how to give value to this difference, proposing women's attitudes and behaviours as positive models for men too.

The woman soldier and the patriotic woman are both stereotype images, which ignore major aspects of the everyday life of the women supposed to fit them. Women who try to live within either role are constrained and bound to suffer.

When praising the independent and competent life of the woman soldier one should not ignore the high personal price paid for the conquest of equality. The Tailhook scandal – when it became known that collective rituals bordering on rape were regarded as normal treatments reserved by male marines for their female colleagues – are only the tip of an iceberg of daily difficulties, and of what amounts essentially to rejection of women by broad sectors of the armed forces. The authoritarian atmosphere and the rituals through which internal hierarchies are established are foreign to traditional female experience and psychology. The military life further involves frequent, sudden geographical movements, hard to reconcile with conjugal life, and necessarily involves even simple daily activities, like eating in the common mess, which in civilian life occur within the walls of the home. If reconciling military and family life is hard for men, it is even harder for women, especially mothers. Assimilating to a role made to measure for young men is a path many women take because it looks better than others, but it contains aspects they would certainly rather do without.

The traditional woman, especially in its patriotic version, is a woman deprived of and in need of a free, autonomous existence in the world. Meekness, capacity for mediation and dialogue, ability to listen, cannot be valued as long as they are mandatory behaviour for the weak, with no other choice available. A proof of this is in the wives of American soldiers stationed in Europe in the 1960s – masterfully described in, for instance, M. E. Wertsh's book *Military Brats*, about the daily life on base and its effects on the education of soldiers' sons and daughters. The life of these women was caught up in the military system. Those women experienced in more dramatic fashion the oppression and the loneliness of other housewives. The isolation was increased by continual transfers from one place to another, their oppression was compounded with the need to obey unwritten rules governing, for example, the right length for their sons' hair. The patriotic woman suffered neuroses and anguishes, perpetuating them in her children along with the system of patriotic values. The collective economic and political weakness, in which the existence of a solely male army places all women, cannot be removed by declaring that war is men's business, or women will find themselves again and again impotently involved in and dramatically marked by the military and by wars.

It is therefore not possible to assert simplistically that the traditional woman is a bearer of values of peace and that the woman soldier is a woman who abandons what is specifically feminine and yields herself to the needs of male military organization. Nor it is possible to claim that a woman soldier enjoys the same independence and privileges as men. Both represent a militarized femininity and, though in different ways, serve the needs of the military and are both largely a projection of a male need. They are acceptable only as long as they are useful to a masculine order: as long as they do not disturb or question it.

Today there seem to exist only two alternatives for women: acceptance of the traditional model of the patriotic woman, or assimilation to the alternative offered by the traditional image of a soldier. Neither is a satisfactory solution for women. Neither of these choices, clearly, can be incorporated within the system of values and goals sustained by the new women's political movements. Neither can be proposed as a solution. A military persona which can comfortably fit a woman as well as a man is yet to be developed. But nothing less is needed by women.

The existence of a male army changes the power relationships between men and women to the detriment of the latter, in both economic and symbolic terms. Individual women have realized that in peacetime the military career represents a job opportunity, a possibility of income, a possibility of acquiring professional skills for later sale on the civilian market, and status. Some of them, too, are perhaps, like men, attracted by the myth of the 'warrior', but want to live it in their own persons rather than through the intermediary of a husband. Some may be attracted by the mirage of being part of adventures in which they can finally display their prowess and courage, not just their sweetness and beauty. For whatever reason women who become soldiers choose to do so, among all the options open to them – and the women are almost universally volunteers – it would be an act of paternalism to deny them the right to make this choice and denounce it as mere assimilation. Once women have joined the armed forces, it clearly benefits them that there should be strict respect for formal equality. Women in the armed forces, for instance, complain of the use of supposedly protective regulations like exclusion from combat to limit their career possibilities. Such regulations implicitly exclude them from the higher ranks in the hierarchy, keeping them in subordinate positions within the armed forces themselves.

Assimilation, understood as women fitting in with the male model, is a process under way in all sections of societies, and it does not so far seem to correspond with parallel assimilation of men to female models and values.

This implies that a civil society which, overall, is taking up a more 'masculine' character, is becoming competitive, hierarchical, aggressive and rigid – turning away from the values that women have historically been the depositaries of. The presence of values like solidarity, meekness, mediation and caring abilities is becoming ever rarer: society is beginning to progressively deny them in both men and women. The 'neutral but male' society emerging seems to be more violent, less civil, further from peace. Assimilation is a source of unease and suffering, both for the women assimilating and for society as a whole. A culture of peace cannot do without the contribution from the values traditionally associated with femininity. Feminine traits – the female 'difference' – cannot and must not be lost.

This book is born of the unease these thoughts have caused its editors, and of the attempt to analyse it after gathering specific evidence on the experiences of women soldiers and their multiple consequences. The intent is primarily cognitive, though with the hope of making a positive contribution to the development of policies that take into account these experiences.

The articles making up this volume are a reworking of the papers presented in a Conference at the European University Institute in 1991. The Conference was part of a broader project directed by the three editors on the theme of the woman soldier and supported by the Forum on the Problems of Peace and War, Florence.

The book highlights a number of specific points: we wished to verify the costs and benefits of female participation in the military for individual women and for women as a whole, in economic, political and citizenship terms. We have accordingly asked what impels some women to a seek a military career, the specific effects of their assimilation into the military, and the strategies through which they face and respond to this situation.

As far as the armed forces are concerned, we wanted to understand the reasons impelling them to enrol women, in the context of a general change, and to enquire whether and why women constitute a disturbing factor; whether women are among the causes of change in military structures or are assimilated without trace.

We then asked how far this experience changes ancient images of women in relation to war and how the new images interact with the traditional ones. Since the new image of the woman soldier has in large part been forged by the media in the context of the Gulf War, and since the Gulf War dramatically highlighted the contrasts and asymmetries between the two images of femininity, the Arab woman in her veil and the

Western woman in uniform, some articles pay particular attention to that experience, which others leave out entirely.

The questions raised in the research project called for answers from the viewpoints of various disciplines. The editors considered the economic, political and symbolic aspects of the problem. In the first section, constituting the general background for the more detailed studies, Elisabetta Addis, an economist, describes the economic choices available to women opting to be soldiers and supplies the information for calculating the economic loss that women as a whole suffer for being excluded from such a major public-expenditure programme as the military budget. Lorenza Sebesta, who specializes in security studies, sets the issue of women in the armed forces in the context of the question of the legitimacy of the use of force by the state. Valeria Russo, a philosopher, studies the mythic image of the woman warrior and the relations between that image and the construction of a 'gender-enemy'. Patricia Hanna, a clinical social worker and consultant at US Navy bases, explains the mechanisms governing personal interactions in the armed forces, the stress factors resulting for women from insertion as a minority into a hierarchical, authoritarian structure, and the strategies American female soldiers – the most numerous group – deploy in order to endure within the military organization.

The second part contains contributions based on the Gulf War and its media representation in order to analyse how gender-images and gender-relationships were modified thereby. Cynthia Enloe, a political scientist, explains how the role of female soldiers first in the invasion of Panama, and subsequently in the Gulf War, has changed the prospects and problems for women who were struggling for equal opportunity in the American armed forces. A very special war – given its technological 'cleanness' and the absence, imposed by the Saudis, of alcohol and prostitution at the bases – rendered definitively acceptable the notion of professionalism of the soldier's trade, applicable to women too. Julie Wheelwright, a journalist, examines the way the media constructed information on women soldiers in a war whose 'visibility' was subject to the narrow filter of the Allied Command on the one side and was openly in the hands of the regime in Iraq. She shows how the media reforged the stereotypes of femininity, using the presence of women to strengthen the image of a 'just war', and how the presence of women affected the debate on the war.

Two case studies at the end of the book consider two anomalous national experiences. Maria Graeff-Wassink, a Westerner and sociologist of the Arab countries, in her article describes the Women's Military Academy in Libya. Contrary to the suspicion with which Western feminists consider the position of the Islamic woman, she gives a largely positive assessment of it. Virgilio Ilari, a jurist and historian of military organization, reconstructs the legislative debate on female military service in Italy – the only NATO country with no women soldiers – from the time of the Constituent Assembly to the present. It emerges clearly from this article that women were denied access to the armed forces because of the slowness, inefficiency and stagnation of the political system, not because of active opposition by the military hierarchies or by pacifist forces.

The book is accompanied by a bibliography which is built primarily around the themes dealt with in the articles, and accordingly concentrates on literature concerning women in the armed forces. Given the inadequacy of bibliographical instruments on topics relating to 'women and war' as a whole, the bibliography also refers to some now-classic titles on related topics not dealt with specifically in the text but in some way connected with it. It refers chiefly to two major lines of study, that on 'women and fighting' which includes examination of the role of women in civil wars as well as in traditional wars and is particularly rich in studies on women in the two world wars, and that on 'women and pacifism'.

This book endeavours to supply data and arguments useful to the debate on female military service, bringing out more clearly aspects and problems connected with women soldiers. It does not aim at supplying a prescription of the most appropriate policies. The editors themselves have different opinions on whether and how female military service ought to be introduced in Italy. However, since policy prescriptions will eventually be the outcome of this debate, we feel it appropriate at least to give a few broad indications. As we said at the outset, it appears from this research that both exclusion from the military and participation in it, though both having positive aspects, have heavy costs for women. The first set of policy indications calls for adopting provisions that limit those costs, by eroding the exclusion and making the integration easier. One indirect way of limiting the exclusion is, for example, the opening to civilians and hence to women of functions that are only indirectly military within the armed forces. Meteorology, cartography, military health, military justice and part of training may be performed by civilians on behalf of the armed forces. In order to facilitate integration it is necessary to accompany the introduction of voluntary female military service – in full legal parity between men and women – with measures and structures to minimize the human costs for women. Committees or other bodies with checking powers, consisting also of civilian women – as already exist in some countries – should be built or strengthened. They should be able to act as a reference point, collect and convey the needs and complaints of the women recruits and prevent and repress any abuses, promoting mutual integration of women and the armed forces. These bodies ought to take due account of the experiences of female soldiers in other countries, in order to improve the quality of female military service.

As clearly emerges from the contributions making up this volume, this issue with its manifold facets cannot be ignored and repressed by the women's movement as a troublesome exception: in the interest of women, it must be faced. It is also clear that the opposition remains between the image of the woman soldier assimilated to the male model, the ultimate limit of the equality policy, and the image of traditional woman whose femininity reflects the soldier's masculinity by inverting it. The ideology of professionalism superficially reconciles them, but the mutual unease between women in the armed forces will not disappear in the near future. Women's different traits must be much more openly deployed, and relationships between the sexes in society as a whole changed much more radically, before a tension like this one can be fully resolved.

Florence
April 1993

E. A.
V. E. R.
L. S.

Part I

Women Soldiers: Economic, Theoretical-Political and Psychological Questions

1 Women and the Economic Consequences of Being a Soldier

Elisabetta Addis

1. INTRODUCTION

In 1990 there were 456,840 women directly employed by armed forces throughout the world. Of these, the vast majority were in the armies of Western, industrialized countries, which may be classified as 'rich' in terms of income per capita and other indicators. Women are not drafted in any country with the exception of Israel. Even in countries where men are conscripted, women are admitted to the service on a volunteer basis. To a very large extent, therefore, women who are soldiers choose to be soldiers.

When given the choice, some women decide to be soldiers with the same freedom, in the same framework of individual rights and liberties as others choose to be janitors, nurses or university teachers. They believe it is better for them to be soldiers than anything else. It is this choice which is the starting point of this paper: a choice which deserves an explanation.

In women's politics, the issue of female participation in the armed forces is controversial. Feminist movements and anti-militaristic movements often share a similar cultural background. In a country like Italy, for example, where women are not admitted in the armed forces, some feminists in the the peace movement do not consider it as an equal-opportunity issue. They give a positive value to the exclusion and oppose opening the armed forces to women. They argue that feminine culture is – willy-nilly – a culture of communication and compromise rather than one of armed conflict.

But, if some women would choose to be soldiers, denying them this possibility is very much a paternalistic position: it

3

implies that somebody other than they knows better than women what is good for them. It asks women to sacrifice whatever individual opportunities they expected to find in military service and whatever collective advantage they might gain by participating in it, for the sake of a common good. It deprives individual women of economic opportunities and it keeps women as a whole in a condition of economic disadvantage in society.

Before taking a position on this issue, I felt I needed more information on facts rather than on matters of principle. As an economist, I wanted to understand and possibly measure the quantities involved. How large is the economic gain in being a soldier, and what economic loss is incurred if women are not allowed to join in the armed forces? In this paper I set myself the task of enquiring into the economic motivations and consequences of entering the armed forces, and the costs and the benefits of being a soldier, both for individual women and for women as a whole. The main point which emerges from the economic analysis of this issue is that participation in the armed forces is an equal-opportunity issue for women in all of society, not only for women who are or wish to be soldiers.

At the individual level, the economic advantage of a woman's choosing to serve in the armed forces depends largely on the differential in wages and employment that women experience in the civilian labour market. The military is an equal-opportunity employer in terms of wages. Women's wages for comparable jobs in the civilian labour market are lower, and female unemployment is, in most countries, higher than male unemployment. A job in the armed forces, therefore, is a better opportunity for a woman than for a man.

At the macroeconomic level, the armed forces may be treated as a very large public expenditure programme, which offers employment and training. In the civilian labour market, where interchangeability of male and female work is less than perfect, an increase in male employment determines an increase in male wages. In addition, the skills acquired in soldiering may increase veterans' wages. The exclusion of women from the armed forces helps to perpetuate employment and wage differentials in favour of men.

Computed from the point of view of the economist, the gain of being a soldier may be quite large for the individual woman. Certainly the collective economic loss when women are not allowed in armies is much larger than the sum of individual losses. Exclusion from the military fosters the economic disavantage of women in the civilian sector as well.

Economic considerations are not the only factor that matters in the issue of preparing for war. Other moral, political and strategic considerations may apply. While it may be found that the benefits outweigh the costs, it does not necessarily follow that women – or men for that matter – should be soldiers. But a policy of peace cannot ignore the structure of material incentives that weigh on men and women and affect their choices. Women's politics cannot ignore the issue of economic equality, and inequality within the army generates economic inequality in society.

I will present my considerations according to the lines along which economists usually think: microeconomic considerations when dealing with the problem of individual choice under constraints, and macroeconomic considerations when dealing with the problem of the overall distribution of economic resources.

In this research, I faced a formidable paucity of data suitable for economic analysis. Data on military employment come from military sources. Two were particularly useful: the WEU (Western European Union) Report submitted by B. Baarveld-Schlaman[1] and two booklets issued by NATO (North Atlantic Treaty Organization).[2]

Data on military wages in comparison with civilian wages for the same level of instruction were not available for most countries. The relative wage of military personnel, veterans and non-veterans, was widely studied in the USA.[3] In Europe, though, there is very little, if any, research done on the economic effects of the armed forces on wages and employment. The question of how economically advantageous it is to be a soldier in Europe for men, let alone women, remains unanswered. It was impossible for me to begin collecting country-by-country data on civilian military wage differentials alone.

Notwithstanding this limitation, I hope to have been able, in this paper, to marshal the scant evidence about women soldiers and to clarify the most important economic issues connected with women's participation in the armed forces.

The structure of the paper is as follows. Part 1 is descriptive and examines the available information about women in the armed forces. Parts 2 and 3 deal with the problems of individual choice. I will argue that, although being a soldier may not be better than a comparable job for the average man, and although the cost of being a soldier may be higher for women than for men because soldiering is a 'male' activity, women are at such a disadvantage in terms of wages and employment that their wish to be enrolled is justified. Part 4 deals with the problem of reallocation of resources through military spending. I argue that military spending is equivalent to a very large public expenditure programme which introduces a strong bias in production and in the wage and employment structures, often to the detriment of women and to the activities that they would rather see financed. Part 5 contains my conclusions.

2.   WOMEN IN THE ARMED FORCES

Table 1.1 presents the total number of women and men employed in world's armed forces, country by country. Women soldiers account for 456,840 out of a total number of 25,381,960. These numbers were compiled by myself using *The Military Balance*[4] as a source. The counting is somewhat biased because *The Military Balance* is itself a compilation, and if the original source omitted to mention women, they have remained omitted. In particular, Israel and the Soviet Union, who employ women in their forces, were not included and the 1990 figures for these two countries are not yet available. Swedish women soldiers were also omitted: the Swedish Forsvarsstaben, Ministry of Defence, kindly and promptly provided the number. The total number of women soldiers therefore may be about half a million, i.e. less than 2 per cent of the total.

Most women soldiers are employed by NATO countries. Australia, Brunei, China, Cyprus and South Africa are the non-NATO countries that count women among their soldiers. The country with the highest absolute number of women soldiers is the USA, followed by China, Great Britain, France and Cyprus respectively. Other countries have less than 10,000 women soldiers each.

Table 1.1 Women Soldiers in the World

Country	Total number of soldiers	Number of women soldiers
Afghanistan	58,000	
Albania	48,000	
Algeria	125,500	
Angola	100,000	
Argentina	75,000	
Australia	68,100	7,500
Austria	42,500	
Bahamas	2,750	
Bahrain	6,000	
Bangladesh	10,300	
Belgium	92,000	3,200
Belize	760	
Benin	4,350	
Bolivia	28,000	
Botswana	4,500	
Brazil	324,200	
Brunei	9,200	250
Bulgaria	129,000	
Burkina Faso	8,700	
Burma	230,000	
Burundi	7,200	
Cambodia	111,800	
Cameroon	11,600	
Canada	90,000	7,700
Cape Verde	1,300	
C.A.R.	6,500	
Chad	17,000	
Chile	95,800	
China	3,030,000	136,000
Colombia	136,000	
Congo	3,800	
Costa Rica	7,800	
Cote d'Ivoire	7,100	
Cuba	180,500	
Cyprus	10,400	200
Czechoslovakia	198,200	
Denmark	31,700	900
Djibouti	4,100	
Domenican Republic	22,800	
Ecuador	57,800	
Egypt	450,000	
El Salvador	44,600	
Equatorial Guinea	1,300	
Ethiopia	438,000	
Fiji	5,000	
Finland	31,000	

Table 1.1   (cont.)

Country	Total number of soldiers	Number of women soldiers
France	461,250	13,300
Gabon	9,750	
Gambia	900	
Germany E	137,700	
Germany W	469,000	
Ghana	12,200	
Greece	162,500	3,400
Guatemala	43,300	
Guinea	9,700	
Guinea-Bissau	9,200	
Guyana	1,950	
Haiti	7,400	
Honduras	18,200	
Hungary	94,000	
Iceland	0	
India	1,262,000	
Indonesia	283,000	
Iran	504,000	
Iraq	1,000,000	
Ireland	13,000	90
Israel[1]	141,000	
Italy	389,600	
Jamaica	3,350	
Japan	249,000	
Jordan	85,250	
Kenya	23,600	
Korea (North)	1,111,000	
Korea (South)	750,000	
Kuwait	20,300	
Laos	55,100	
Lebanon	0	
Lesotho	2,000	
Liberia	7,800	
Libya[2]	85,000	
Luxembourg	800	
Madagascar	21,000	
Malawi	7,250	
Malaysia	129,500	
Mali	7,300	
Malta	1,500	
Mauritania	11,100	
Mexico	148,500	
Mongolia	21,500	
Morocco	192,500	
Mozambique	72,000	
Namibia	0	

Table 1.1 (*cont.*)

Country	Total number of soldiers	Number of women soldiers
Nepal	35,000	
Netherlands	102,600	1,700
New Zealand	11,600	
Nicaragua	63,500	
Niger	3,300	
Nigeria	94,500	
Norway	34,100	
Oman	29,500	
Pakistan	550,000	
Panama	12,250	
Papua New Guinea	3,500	
Paraguay	16,000	
Peru	120,000	
Philippines	108,500	
Poland	312,800	
Portugal	68,000	
Qatar	7,500	
Romania	143,000	
Rwanda	5,200	
Saudi Arabia	67,500	
Senegal	9,700	
Seychelles	1,300	
Sierra Leone	3,150	
Singapore	55,500	
Somali Republic	64,500	
South Africa	77,400	3,200
Soviet Union[3]	3,988,000	
Spain	274,500	200
Sri Lanka	22,000	
Sudan	75,700	
Suriname	3,000	
Sweden[4]	64,500	27,000
Switzerland	3,500	
Syria	40,400	
Taiwan	370,000	
Tanzania	46,800	
Thailand	283,000	
Togo	5,900	
Trinidad	2,650	
Tunisia	38,000	
Turkey	647,400	
Uganda	70,000	
United Arab Emirates	49,000	
United Kingdom	306,000	18,000
United States	2,117,900	216,000
Uruguay	25,200	

Table 1.1   (cont.)

Country	Total number of soldiers	Number of women soldiers
Venezuela	71,000	
Vietnam	1,052,000	
Yemen N	38,500	
Yemen S	27,500	
Yugoslavia	180,000	
Zaire	61,000	
Zambia	16,200	
Zimbabwe	54,600	
Total	26,332,310	446,840

Notes
[1] In Israel young women who have no children may be conscript. The exact number of women soldiers was not reported in any available source. Upon request, the Defence Department sent me informative booklets in Hebrew, but no exact number.
[2] There is a special academy for selected women officers in Libya (cf. M. Graeff-Wassink's (Chapter 7) contribution.) The exact number is not known, but is very small. The Defence Department did not reply to direct enquiry.
[3] In the Soviet Union women with special skills (physicians, logisticians, etc.) can volunteer. Direct enquiry on the exact number found no reply.
[4] The source of this number is a direct reply from the Swedish Defence Department, which we wish to thank for the cooperation.

Source   International Institute for Strategic Studies, *The Military Balance* (London, 1990).

Approximately 60 per cent of all women soldiers are employed by the NATO Forces. In non-NATO countries, China – a relatively poor country in terms of income per capita – has the largest number of women soldiers. All other non-NATO countries that employ women in their forces, including Brunei, are in the upper part of world income distribution. For a number of social and cultural factors, Australia and (white) South Africa are akin to the NATO countries. Cyprus is culturally and geopolitically close to Mediterranean countries, of which only those who belong to NATO accept women (and a bit reluctantly at that), so it is somewhat surprising that it allows women in its armed forces. Brunei would merit a case study, to understand why and how women become soldiers there.

Because of the centrality of NATO countries, I will concentrate on information available for NATO and Western European Union countries.

In most of these countries, women entered the armed forces in the 1970s. Nationally compiled information materials sometimes make references to mythical women warriors of the past, or present women soldiers as the heirs of some former paramilitary support organization. However, the real implementation of present policies dates no further back than the last two decades.

Fourteen out of sixteen NATO countries allow women in the armed forces. Only Italy and Iceland (which does not have an army) do not allow women soldiers. Table 1.2 shows the number of men and women in the armed forces of each NATO country and their rank in 1990. There are minor discrepancies between these figures and those found in *The Military Balance*.

Table 1.3 contains information about the various policies followed in each country. Curiously, Turkey accepts women only as officers while Luxembourg accepts only enlisted women. It would be interesting to study the rationale behind these policies in more detail.[5]

As already mentioned, although most NATO countries have compulsory service requirements for men, women are admitted only as volunteers. The rationale behind this is not difficult to see: it is impossible to conscript young mothers, on the grounds that their children need them; and if only young non-mothers are drafted it is not difficult to forecast an increase in the fertility rate of young women. Many women may choose to be mothers rather than soldiers: many men, if they had the choice, would undoubtedly do the same. In Israel, demographic growth is an official policy, and many incentives, besides non-conscription, are offered to parents.

The length of service is the same for both sexes, except in Greece. In Turkey training is different for women, and so is non-basic training and training of officers in Greece and Spain.

In these last two countries parental leave is not provided, and in Spain pregnancy regulations do not provide for retention. This is quite peculiar, given the fact that the Spanish entry in the NATO booklet boasts perfect equality including the controversial participation in combat.[6] Then again there are only 96 women in the Spanish armed forces,

Table 1.2   Women Soldiers in NATO Countries (31 Dec. 1990)

	Nether-lands	Norway	Portugal	Spain	Turkey	United Kingdom	United States
1.a. Total men and women in the Armed Forces	95,723	40,637	64,318	230,470	598,856	303,003	2,034,354
Army	60,122	21,784	33,740	169,376	488,157	150,223	691,096
Air Force	16,467	8,673	14,139	25,790	58,265	88,356	493,675
Navy	14,611	9,987	16,439	29,889	52,434	61,851	738,670
Nursing Corps	4,523			5,425		2,573	110,913
1.b. Total men and women less compulsory/con-scripts in the Armed Forces	52,840	14,878	29,947	59,668	85,330	Same as above	Same as above
Army	23,187	6,631	10,907	35,241	44,274		
Air Force	12,833	4,766	8,901	11,804	26,271		
Navy	13,111	3,286	10,139	11,836	14,785		
Nursing Corps	3,709			5,425			
2. Total women in the Armed Forces	2,795	972	14	96	152	17,747	223,297
Army	1,188	452	6	3	106	5,523	69,349
Air Force	508	315	8	5	24	6,521	60,271
Navy	836	199		1	22	3,321	57,698
Nursing Corps	263			87		2,382	35,979
3. Total no. of women officers Armed Forces	356	526	14	87	152	2,530	34,104
Army	175	240	6	1	106	582	8,906
Air Force	107	189	8	-	24	896	9,133
Navy	70	96		-	22	311	6,301
Nursing Corps	4			86		741	9,764
4. Total no. of enlisted women Armed Forces	2,439	78		9		15,217	189,193
Army	1,013	33		2		4,941	60,443
Air Force	401	28		5		5,625	51,138
Navy	766	17		1		3,010	51,397
Nursing Corps	259			1		1,641	26,215

so if they renounce childbearing it will probably not endanger the population. Turkey, which is the least egalitarian country in its treatment of male and female soldiers, has a different retirement regulation for women.

Table 1.2 *(cont.)*

	Belgium	Canada	Denmark	France	Germany	Greece	Luxembourg
1.a. Total men and women in							
the Armed Forces	86,868	85,606	30,542	550,000	433,450	161,500	700
Army	58,418	(unified	18,627	293,000	303,220	121,000	
Air Force	18,502	military	8,738	94,000	94,830	22,500	
Navy	4,522	includes	5,177	66,000	35,400	18,000	
Nursing Corps	5,326	nurses)					
1.b. Total men and women less compulsory/conscripts in the							
Armed Forces	51,924	85,606	19,612	291,000	199,680 ⎫		
Army	33,159		9,046	110,000	120,430 ⎪	Same	Same
Air Force	13,662		6,070	58,000	56,990 ⎬	as above	as above
Navy	2,951		4,496	46,000	22,260 ⎭		
Nursing Corps	2,152						
2. Total women in the							
Armed Forces	3,092	9,056	1,025	20,000	462	4,671	28
Army	1,699		411	8,500	310	2,284	
Air Force	894		403	5,900	101	1,266	
Navy	217		211	1,500	51	1,121	
Nursing Corps	282			2,900			
3. Total no. of women officers							
Armed Forces	139	1,788	47	1,150	289	451	N/A
Army	75		27	300	223	259	
Air Force	31		17	200	37	107	
Navy	8		3	50	29	85	
Nursing Corps	25			550			
4. Total no. of enlisted women							
Armed Forces	2,953	7,268	978	2,000	173	4,224	28
Army	1,624		384	1,056	87	2,025	
Air Force	863		386	185	64	1,163	
Navy	209		208	107	22	1,036	
Nursing Corps	257			365			

Source NATO, *Women in NATO* (Brussels, 1991).

Pay, on the other hand, appears to be the same for men and women of the same rank in all nations. Women may be prevented by direct or indirect regulations from attaining senior grades (the exclusion from 'combat' is one such

Table 1.3 Policies Concerning Women Soldiers in NATO Countries (31 Dec. 1990)

	BE	CA	DE	FR	GE	GR	IT	LU	IIU	NO	PO	SP	IU	UK	US
1. Legislation which prohibits discrimination on basis of gender?	Yes	Yes	Yes	Yes	Yes	Yes	Yes	Yes	Yes	Yes	Yes	Yes	Yes	Yes	Yes
2. Does the legislation apply within the armed forces?	Yes	Yes	Yes	Yes	Yes	Yes	N/A	Yes	Yes	Yes	Yes	Yes	Yes	Yes	Yes
3. Combat exlusion legislation or policies on women in armed forces?															
a. Legislation	No	No	No	No	Yes	No	N/A	No	No	No	No	No	No	No	Yes
b. Policies	No	No	No	Yes	Yes	Yes	N/A	No	Yes	No	No	No	Yes	Yes	Yes
4. Armed force initiatives to expand role of women in military	No	Yes	Yes	Yes	Yes	Yes	N/A	No	Yes	Yes	Yes	Yes	Yes	Yes	Yes
5. Service in armed forces	Comp	Vol	Comp & Vol	Comp	Comp & Vol	Comp	Comp	Vol & Vol	Comp	Comp & Vol	Comp & Vol	Comp	Comp	Vol	Vol
6. Women's Service in armed forces	Vol	Vol	Vol	Vol	Vol	Vol	Excl	Vol	Vol	Vol	Vol	Vol	Vol	Vol	Vol
7. Women's length of service in armed forces different from men?	No	No	No	No	No	Yes	N/A	No	No	No	No	No	No	No	No

Table 1.3 (cont.)

	BE	CA	DE	FR	GE	GR	IT	LU	IIU	NO	PO	SP	IU	UK	US
8. Training for female officers different from male officers?							N/A								
a. Basic training	No	No	No	No	No	No		No	No	No	No	No	No	No	No
b. Other	No	No	No	No	No	Yes		No	No	No	No	No	No	No	No
9. Training for enlisted women different from enlisted men?							N/A								
a. Basic training	No	No	No	No	No	No		No	No	No	No	Yes	No	No	
b. Other	No	No	No	No	No	Yes		No	No	No	No	Yes	No	No	
10. Discipline regulations for women different from men?	No	No	No	No	No	No	N/A	No	No	Yes	No	No	No	No	No
11. Pay for women different from men?	No	No	No	No	No	No	N/A	No	No	No	No	No	No	No	No
12. Pregnancy regulations provide for retention?	Yes	Yes	Yes	Yes	Yes	Yes	N/A	No	Yes	Yes	Yes	No	Yes	Yes	Yes

N/A = Not applicable

Table 1.3 (cont.)

	BE	CA	DE	FR	GE	GR	IT	LU	IIU	NO	PO	SP	IU	UK	US
13. Parental regulations provide for paternal/maternal leave?	Yes	Yes	Yes	Yes	Yes	No	Yes	No	Yes	Yes	Yes	No	Yes	Yes	Yes
14. Child care provisions in regulations?	No	No	No	Yes	No	No	No	Yes	No	No	Yes	Yes	Yes	No	Yes
15. Retirement regulations different from men?	No	No	No	No	No	No	N/A	No	No	No	No	No	Yes	No	No
16. Numbers of women in Armed Forces expected to increase/decrease/no change?	No Change	Inc	Inc	Inc	Inc	Inc	N/A	Inc	Inc	Inc	Inc	Inc	Inc	Inc	Dec
17. Percentage of women in Armed Forces expected to increase/decrease/no change	No Change	Inc	Inc	Inc	Inc	Inc	N/A	Inc	Inc	Inc	Inc	Inc	Inc	Inc	No Change
18. Top female grade serving at present (use NATO grade)	OF2	OF6	OF3	OF6	OF5	OF5	N/A	OR3	OF4	OF3	OF4	OF1	OF5	OF6	OF8

Inc = Increase Dec = Decrease
Source NATO, *Women in NATO* (Brussels, 1991).

indirect regulation), but ordering by 'rank' seems to override ordering by 'gender': it is grades and seniority that determine wages. This, I believe, is a key point in understanding the economics of women soldiers.

3. THE COST OF BEING A SOLDIER: WOMEN SOLDIERS IN AUTHORITARIAN ARMED FORCES

If women, or men for that matter, become soldiers they must be persuaded that the cost is worth the benefits.

I suggest that the direct cost of becoming a soldier may be higher for young women than for young men, and the cost of being a soldier may be higher, for both sexes, than the cost of other jobs requiring the same amount of time and effort. The relative advantage of being a soldier is greater for a woman because women are at a disadvantage in the civilian labour market and this relative advantage is large enough to offset the costs.

There are costs that make soldiering a harder job than most, for men as well as for women. Apart from the risk of being mobilized in the event of war, even in peacetime being a soldier is hard on family life, due to the constraints of barracks life, the possibility of relocation and overseas assignments. The infringment of military life on personal life is usually harder on mothers than on fathers because of the different parental role they are usually expected to take.

In addition, sources seem to point in particular to a cost which is difficult to quantify.[7] This is the cost that derives from the masculinity of the traditional military authoritarian model, which affects also men, but particularly women.

Most people would agree that the army is a 'male' institution: more so than the judiciary, the university system, or other institutions which historically were also built and inhabited only by men. It is difficult however to pinpoint why it is that the army is more male than the university: masculinity, like femininity, is a complex cultural construct rather than a simple function of our biological sex.[8]

The masculinity of the armed forces is reflected not only in the fact that they must be ready to fight, but also in that, in peacetime, they are governed by the twin mechanisms of hierarchy and authority to a much greater extent than any other institution. Psychological research seems to indicate that men are more likely than women to establish a ranking in relationships.[9] Among young men, admission to an established group of higher-ranking individuals sometimes may even take the form of cruel initiation rites. But even in daily relations, the process of establishing authority and submitting to it seems more familiar to the males of the human race. Women entering the Army sometimes experience a 'culture shock' when they have to learn the unfamiliar ropes of establishing a ranking, and of maintaining the proper relations of authority.

Physical prowess has an important role in this ranking process. Women are at a biological disadvantage in this field. By proving their physical adequacy, moreover, men can hope to gain a prized confirmation of their own manhood. Proving her 'manhood', of course, only casts on a woman a scornful, suspicious shadow.

It should be noted, also, that when armed forces are comprised of all or mostly volunteers, any undue hardship, humiliating training, or abuse of authority must be, literally, compensated with higher military wages if they are to continue recruiting. The environment in a force comprised mostly of draftees is likely to be different, therefore, from that in an all-volunteer force.

In addition, the sophisticated technology of modern weaponry requires an educated personnel and a continuous flow of information between the lower ranks and the decision-makers. This contrasts with the one-way flow of information (orders to the subordinates) of traditional hierarchical ranking. The armed forces may therefore be evolving towards a less authoritarian model of internal behaviour. This evolution may change the masculine cultural climate and render them more tolerant of a feminine presence.

4.   THE BENEFITS OF BEING A SOLDIER

The change to a professional, less authoritarian, force has helped create a growing perception of soldiering as a career not unlike any other. Through the 1980s, despite the wave of *Rambo* and *Top Gun* movies trying to revive the myth of the armed man as a superhuman hero, soldiering lost some of its symbolic allure as the proof of one's masculinity, and is increasingly perceived as just another job to be done.

A prospective job is usually evaluated first and foremost from the economic viewpoint, taking into consideration the wage, the training and the derived opportunities for future employment. Many men and women may nowadays perceive soldiering simply as a path to relative emancipation and growth in social status.

Is this perception justified by the actual benefits of being a soldier?

Soldiering, for men, is not a particularly smart career choice. The argument has often been made that military spending is beneficial to the economy. Besides stimulating production, it provides education and skills for soldiers. The veterans can then use them in the civilian labour market to the benefit of all, reaping themselves the fruits of this human capital accumulation in the form of higher wages.

This does not appear to be the case. The most important evidence about the individual advantage and disadvantage of being a soldier was gathered in the United States. There, the existence of a Veterans Administration motivated the collection and analysis of data related to the economic status of veterans in comparison with other men in the same age range who had not been in the service.

It was first submitted that, while Second World War veterans earned comparatively more than non-veterans, the opposite was true for Vietnam War veterans.[10] It was then pointed out that the relative advantage of Second World War veterans was explained entirely by a pre-selection bias:[11] during the Second World War the armed forces selected better-educated young men from a social background of comparative advantage. If their subsequent job and wage performance is matched with that of comparable non-veterans the advantage disappears or becomes slightly negative.

Further research conducted by J. Angrist[12] confirms that the relatively low job market performance of Vietnam War veterans was due to an initial negative bias in recruitment.

However, the educational benefits of the Veterans Administration did improve the skills, wages and employment levels of the veterans. Interestingly, those who benefited most were the most educated: college-educated veterans benefited more than those who were educated to high school level, and these, in turn, benefited more than unskilled personnel.

In general, therefore, it seems that being a soldier was not the smartest choice a man could make within the labour market structure. It was equally comparable to other available choices and, in order to be rewarding for a man, probably required a particular taste for becoming a soldier.

All these comparisons, however, were made with no distinction as to the sex of the soldiers, as there were not very many women in the armed forces. Before the Second World War women were only in auxiliary service. About 350,000 women served during the war, and they then decreased in number and capacities until the 1970s; in the Vietnam era they made up only 2 per cent of the total. The fact that being a soldier is not a smart career move for a man does not imply that it is not a smart career choice for a woman. In the USA the earning ratio is about 0.66, i.e. on average women earn less than 70 per cent of what men earn.[13] The wage differential needs to be adjusted to take account of the fact that women have more and/or different training, and different patterns of seniority because they temporarily stop working at childbearing age and because they move to follow their husbands. Nonetheless, a gap of about 20 per cent still holds for men and women with comparable training and experience.[14]

Army recruiting procedures are standardized. Wages are not contracted on an individual basis, but have to be equal for people with the same education and experience. The military wage, therefore, is relatively less discriminatory. This is confirmed by the fact that the quality of female would-be recruits is usually considered satisfactory, even if complaints about the overall quality of recruits are sometimes aired by personnel officers.

In Europe, wage equality probably does not play the same strong role that it does in the USA. Greater unionization of the labour force and the presence of large public sector employment keep the wage differential between sexes relatively lower. However, the unemployment gap between the two sexes is also disturbingly wider.[15] So it is the relative lack of other employment opportunities that keeps the supply of women soldiers higher than the somewhat small demand.

There is, in short, an economic incentive for women to become soldiers, more so than for men, and even if the cost of belonging to such an authoritarian organization may be high. This incentive derives from the fact that women are at a great disadvantage in the civilian labour market.

I do not want to claim here that women are the victim of a 'poverty draft'. The uniform is a choice, it is not an Arab veil, which unwilling women are forced to wear by men. However, it is true that it is not easy to tell the carrot of equal pay in the service from the stick of women's unemployment and lower wages in other jobs.

5.   THE MACROECONOMICS OF MILITARY SPENDING AND WOMEN

The macroeconomics of military spending is by now a large and established field of analysis.[16] Economists have tracked down the effects of military spending on production using different methodologies and disaggregating for different sectors.[17]

National accounting figures in countries where there is conscription adopt the convention of excluding the armed forces from labour force calculations and consequently from the unemployment rate.[18] Most labour economists conduct analyses of the labour market using only civilian labour force figures. However, the armed forces are in many countries one of the largest employers of workers of the male sex. Table 1.4 shows the percentage of the total labour force employed by the army in NATO countries.

A public expenditure programme employing a comparable number of women would, in any country, dramatically decrease women's unemployment rates.

Moreover, a degree of occupational segregation by gender has been found by the most important studies on the topic.

Table 1.4　Personnel in NATO Forces

Country	1970	1975	1980	1985	1987	1988	1989	1990	1991e
(0)	(1)	(2)	(3)	(4)	(5)	(6)	(7)	(8)	(9)

Military (thousand)

Belgium	108	103	108	107	109	110	110	106	104
Denmark	42	34	33	29	28	30	31	31	30
France	571	585	575	563	559	558	554	550	542
Germany	455	491	490	495	495	495	503	545	521
Greece	178	185	186	201	199	199	201	201	204
Italy	522	459	474	504	504	506	506	493	474
Luxembourg	1	1	1	1	1	1	1	1	1
Netherlands	112	107	107	103	106	107	106	104	96
Norway	37	38	40	36	38	40	43	51	..
Portugal	229	104	88	102	105	104	104	87	..
Spain	..	..	356	314	314	304	277	263	268
Turkey	625	584	717	814	879	847	780	769	845
United Kingdom	384	348	330	334	328	324	318	308	298

NATO Europe	..	..	3504	3603	3666	3624	3532	3510	..

Canada	91	78	82	83	86	88	98	87	85
United States	3294	2146	2050	2244	2279	2246	2241	2181	2087

N. America	3385	2224	2132	2327	2365	2334	2329	2268	2172

NATO total	..	..	5636	5930	6031	5958	5861	5778	..

Military and civilian personnel as % of labour force

Belgium	3.1	2.3	2.8	2.8	2.8	2.8	2.8	2.7	2.7
Denmark	2.2	1.8	1.6	1.4	1.3	1.4	1.4	1.4	1.4
France	3.3	3.2	3.0	3.0	2.9	2.9	2.8	2.8	2.7
Germany	2.3	2.5	2.4	2.3	2.3	2.3	2.3	2.6	..
Greece	6.2	6.5	6.1	6.1	5.8	5.6	5.8	5.7	5.8
Italy	2.9	2.5	2.3	2.4	2.3	2.3	2.3	2.3	2.2
Luxembourg	0.9	0.8	0.8	0.9	0.8	0.8	0.8	0.8	0.8
Netherlands	2.9	2.7	2.5	2.2	2.1	2.0	2.0	1.9	1.8
Norway	3.1	2.8	2.6	2.3	2.3	2.4	2.6	2.9	..
Portugal	6.5	2.8	2.3	2.6	2.6	2.5	2.5	2.1	..
Spain	..	..	3.0	2.6	2.4	2.3	2.1	2.0	2.0
Turkey	4.4	3.8	4.8	4.8	5.1	4.8	4.4	4.2	4.6
United Kingdom	2.9	2.5	2.2	1.9	1.8	1.8	1.7	1.7	1.6

NATO Europe	..	..	2.8	2.8	2.7	2.7	2.6	2.6	..

Table 1.4   *(cont.)*

Country (0)	1970 (1)	1975 (2)	1980 (3)	1985 (4)	1987 (5)	1988 (6)	1989 (7)	1990 (8)	1991e (9)
Canada	1.5	1.2	1.0	1.0	1.0	1.0	0.9	0.9	0.9
United States	5.3	3.4	2.8	2.9	2.8	2.7	2.7	2.6	2.5
North America	5.0	3.2	2.6	2.7	2.6	2.5	2.5	2.4	2.3
NATO total	..	..	2.7	2.7	2.7	2.6	2.5	2.5	..

Source   NATO, *Financial and Economic Data relating to NATO Defence*, Dec. 1991.

Therefore there is likely to be, in each market, a classical effect on wages since as the supply of men on the civilian labour market decreases, their relative wage must grow.

Military spending employing only male personnel therefore increases male employment and male wages. I have done some calculations on the Italian wage and employment figures.[19] The most important discovery was that in Italy, for the 14–24-year age range (the age class from which 300,000 are drafted) the draft explained almost all the unemployment differential (14 per cent for boys, not counting the conscripts, and 17.5 per cent for girls). It would take quite a programme of affirmative action to counteract the effects of this.

Finally, we must add the establishment and perpetuation of economic power. This is a concept which is difficult to measure but which closely relates to the influence one acquires when deciding how to spend large amounts of money. A general who decides what to buy for the troops, be it weapons or towels, has an influence on suppliers. His status in society is due not only to his education, his wage and the other perks of his job, but to a very real decision-making power which he exercises, in peacetime as well as during a war, on the surrounding economy. It is the same kind of power and status associated with high level management, chief executives of big corporations for example, in an advanced industrial society.

The exclusion of women from the armed forces or the limitation in number and ranking imposed on women excludes them from this particular source of power.

The existence of armed forces totally or partially closed to women deeply affects the distribution of power and of wealth in the civilian society.

It does not follow from this reasoning, of course, that women should be soldiers or that women who choose to become soldiers do so because they understand the political economy of gender and military spending. However, when trying to devise policies that give men and women equal opportunities, it is important to keep in mind the existence of this channel, the armed forces, through which male opportunities are improved.

6. CONCLUSIONS

In this paper I tried to collect the existing evidence about women soldiers, about the structure of incentives that may have favoured their choice to be soldiers and about the economic consequences, for women, of being or not being part of the armed forces.

My research was severely limited by the fact that, in Europe, little is known about the effects of military employment on the civilian labour market, even for men. Much of my argument was derived from US data only.

At the individual level, the cost for a woman of entering an organization which operates under the unfamiliar mechanism of hierarchy and authority may include a costly adjustment and a revision of traditional roles. Contemporary armed forces, however, because they are in part or completely voluntary, and because they require informational efficiency, tend to be less authoritarian than in the past.

Beyond the variety of individual motivations, the entry of women in the armed forces has been helped by a growing perception of soldiering as a career not unlike any other. Soldiering has lost some of its symbolic allure as the proof of one's masculinity, and has become just a job. The equality of wages and the possibility of training and future employment make the job attractive.

Empirical research conducted in the USA shows, however, that for men, being a veteran did not constitute an advantage in the civilian labour market. It did not compare favourably with other careers requiring comparable training or work effort.

For women, the armed service is still an excellent opportunity, because employment and wages for women in traditional or non-traditional jobs are worse than those of men. The persistent women's disadvantage forms an incentive to choose a relatively egalitarian employer, such as the armed forces.

It may further be argued that in countries where the services are purely male a huge flow of public expenditure – military expenditure – is under exclusively male control and directly benefits, in terms of employment and wages, males alone. Policies designed to create equal opportunities for men and women in the civilian labour market should take into account the fact that they have to counteract a strong bias in favour of men created by military expenditure.

I want to stress the fact that the existence of an armed force comprised exclusively or mostly of men creates and perpetuates economic inferiority among civilian women.

In the Introduction to this book, we contrast two possible images of militarized femininity. One is the traditional woman, on which the military depends as supporting wife, sister and mother of a soldier, as nurse, prostitute near camp, or volunteer in patriotic organizations. The other is the professionalized, competent woman soldier, as has appeared in the Gulf War, ready to fight and kill on order, like a man; and who suffers within a male-dominated force, as in the Tailhook scandal. Both kinds of women help the military system to function. Both roles entail heavy costs for the women who have to fulfill them. The second, however, carries the advantage, for individual women and for women in society, of granting a better economic status and relative economic independence: and this, in my opinion, is an important step towards a world where women's freedom will be more than freedom to choose the least of two evils.

Notes

1. Assembly of Western European Union, *Report: The Role of Women in the Armed Forces*, reported by B. Baarveld-Schlaman (Paris, 1991).
2. NATO, *Women in the NATO Forces* (Brussels, 1986) and NATO, *Women in NATO: 30 years of Progress and Success* (Brussels, 1991).
3. J. D. Angrist, 'The Effect of Veterans Benefits on Veterans' Education and Earnings, *NBER Working Papers*, 3492 (1990) and J. D. Angrist and A. B. Krueger, 'Why do World War II Veterans earn more than non-Veterans?', *NBER Working Papers*, 2991 (1989).
4. International Institute for Strategic Studies, *The Military Balance* (London, 1990).
5. They clearly derive from conflicting views about what is properly feminine. Women cannot be officers because they cannot lead, but they are obedient so they can be enlisted. Women are more educated therefore they can be officers, but they lack the physical strength to be enlisted. This confusion reflects the uneasiness with which armed forces reconcile themselves to the idea of having women in their ranks.
6. NATO, *Women in NATO*.
7. C. Enloe, *Does Khaki Become you?* (London: Pluto Press, 1983) and P. Hanna, 'An Overview of Stressors in the Careers of US Servicewomen', Ch. 4 in this volume.
8. W. Chapkis, 'Sexuality and Militarism', in E. Isaksson (ed.) *Women and the Military System* (London: Harvester Wheatsheaf, 1988) and W. Chapkis, *Loaded Questions: Women in the Military* (Amsterdam: Transnational Institute, 1981).
9. C. Gilligan, *In a Different Voice* (Cambridge, Mass.: Harvard UP, 1985) and D. Tannen, *You Just Don't Understand* (New York: Ballantine, 1990).
10. S. Rosen and P. Taubman, 'Changes in Life Cycle Earnings: What do Social Security Data Show?', *Journal of Human Resources*, 17 (1982) 3, pp. 321–38.
11. Angrist and A. B. Krueger, 'Why do World War II Veterans earn more than non-Veterans?'
12. Angrist, 'The Effect of Veterans' Benefits on Veterans' Education and Earnings'.
13. M. Gunderson, 'Male–Female Wage Differentials and Policy Responses', *Journal of Economic Literature*, March 1989.
14. C. Goldin, *Understanding the Gender Gap* (Oxford: Oxford University Press, 1990).
15. J. Mincer, 'Intercountry Comparisons of Labour Force Trends and of Related Developments: An Overview', *Journal of Labour Economics*, January 1985.

16.   See for example S. Deger and T. Sen, *Military Expenditure: The Political Economy of International Security* (Stockholm: SIPRI, 1990); K. Hartley and T. Sandler (eds) *The Economics of Defence Spending* (London: Routledge, 1990); C. Schmidt and F. Blackaby (eds) *Peace, Defence, and Economic Analysis* (London: Macmillan, 1987).

17.   Some scholars argue that military spending is an ideal stimulus for the economy because it is Keynesian spending in its pure form, with the minimum 'crowding out' of private investment. Others argue that if the private sector had been subsidized by the same amount directly rather than indirectly, the gains in output, employment and productivity due to tecnological change would have been greater. See, for example, L. Dumas (ed.) *The Political Economy of Arms Reduction* (Boulder: Westview, 1982), and Hartley and Sandler (eds) *The Economics of Defence Spending*.

18.   The unemployment rate is computed by surveying a sample of people, and asking them whether they have been looking for a job in the week before the survey; the armed forces are excluded.

19   E. Addis, 'The Effects of Military Spending on Women in Italy' in E. Isaksson (ed.) *Women and the Military System* (London: Harvester Wheatsheaf, 1988).

2 Women and the Legitimation of the Use of Force: The Case of Female Military Service

Lorenza Sebesta

The purpose of this essay is that of analysing the relationship existing between women and the armed forces within the wider context of the question of the legitimacy of the use of force by the state.

My methodological decision is justified by the willingness to broaden the domain of the studies devoted to this argument, not by carrying out an (impossible) synthesis, but by modifying the analytical perspective of the argument itself: while the most widespread objective of the studies that I refer to is that of evaluating the pros and cons of the enrolment of women in an institution considered as an independent variable, the starting point of the present essay is, vice versa, the analysis of this variable.

My enquiry will be centred on the analysis of the 'necessities and choices'[1] that govern the present configuration of the armed forces, intended consequently as dependent variables. Only after having understood the mechanisms that guide such a configuration will it be possible to start thinking of the acceptability of the armed forces as they appear today (necessarily reference will be made to a case study, Italy) and then, eventually, of the opportunity of women being included.

1. THE STATE OF THE ART

Generally speaking, the majority of research conducted in the last twenty years or so on the topic 'women and armed forces' falls into two categories: one that is *descriptive* and one that is *prescriptive*.

Research aiming at the analysis of the condition of women in the armed forces from a sociological, psychological and economic point of view belongs to the *first category*, as well as the contributions of a memorialistic kind, which refer to the experiences of direct or indirect support given by women to the war effort during civil or international conflicts[2] – experiences that refer to two very different realms (war and peace), but according to the point of view of the same institution, the armed forces, and of the same gender, the female.[3]

To the idea of a modernization 'forced upon relationships and gender identities by total warfare'[4] that often emerges from memorialistic accounts, especially those published in the 1970s, and from historical studies on the effect of women's participation in the two world wars,[5] a contradictory view emerged in the 1980s, linked to the development in the feminist field of the 'thought of sexual difference', aiming to question the theory of equality that had been up to then adopted in the analysis of women's war experiences. A more cautious evaluation of the emancipatory value of this experience then emerged, as it was perceived to have merely endorsed male social models. The authors that adopt such a new perspective have also demonstrated how this emancipation was in reality false – it would reveal itself as being temporary ('for the duration' of the conflict) with regards to labour, and partial, because women employed in industry were often called upon to undertake non-qualified and underpaid positions.[6]

Later a slightly more complex interpretation was offered to the public, one that emphasized the problematic opposition between emancipatory tendencies and 'the reconfirmation of a difference that was suffered and capitalized on', of which the experiences of war were the theatre.[7] The focus of research then moved from the impact of war on women (traditionally measured by analysing quantitatively the difference between what was attributed to women before and after the conflicts in the fields of civil rights, welfare politics, employment and wages) to the reorganization that the female gender has undergone during the conflicts according to models functional to the military system, including both innovative and conservative aspects.[8]

On the other hand, on the side of the empirical studies, the thesis by which military service acts simply as an instrument for the 'perpetuation of role' and as being a fundamental 'patriarchal initiatory rite'[9] has left room for the most variegated hypotheses. A new way of handling these topics has emerged from the pages of *Armed Forces and Society*. Based on the theories of Moskos[10] on one side and of Kanter[11] on the other, authors emphasized the progressive change of the model of the American armed forces from 'institutional' to 'occupational' and, within such a mutation, the importance that the structural components have in influencing those who enter – or rather the importance of factors deriving from the form of the organization itself, such as the structure of the opportunities of power and the 'relative number'.[12]

The analysis based on the application of Kanter's model, at first, seemed to comply with the author's conclusions on 'relative numbers' – that state that a small group (15 women against 85 men) in an 'unfamiliar' environment tends to accept the values of the dominant group. More recent empirical studies instead seem to overthrow these conclusions, emphasizing, in the case of military women, an accentuation of the female characteristics instead of, as one would have expected, a process of 'masculinization' or at least of 'androgynization'.[13]

So if the first results seemed to be in favour of a rise in the percentage of women admitted in the armed forces (now over 10 per cent in the United States but much lower percentages in Europe) as a necessary prerequisite for a balanced integration of the two genders, the final hypothesis seems to diminish the reasons for this. One must emphasize, though, that the limited number of samples and of characteristics considered in this kind of analysis (such as masculinization) make generalization very problematic.

The category of *prescriptive* studies refers to the 'necessities' of the subjects, be they a particular category of citizens (women) or an institution (military). Two kinds of analysis belong to this category. The first adopts *gender* as a primary point of reference, emphasizing the political, economic and ethical benefits that women could obtain by gaining access to the military system or by participating in critical moments of war and how such access could change the connotations of the conception of the female gender itself, by, for example, favouring the definite acquisition of the rights connected with full citizenship *(first class citizenship)*; the second, adopting the point of view of the *military institution*, analyses the technical and objective necessities of the armed forces and how they conjugate with the presence of women in the armed forces.

With regard to the first type of analysis (according to the women's point of view) it is well known from Aristotle on, that the concept of 'citizenship' is associated with the right/duty of 'carrying arms' on behalf of the political community;[14] more precisely, from the 1970s on, military service was seen as a potential way for a few minority groups present in the United States to obtain legitimacy and political rights.[15] This has become a recurring theme in literature concerning women and the armed forces, even if, as was correctly emphasized, the transformation of military participation into political legitimization and *first class citizenship* is not really an automatic process.[16]

Moreover, women's access to the armed forces has been seen as a possible means of gaining access to the control of the use of force; such an access would on the one hand lead to a participation in the formation of the norms for its exercise; on the other hand, it would permit women to refuse to delegate their proper defence to an 'external' protector. The adoption of this perspective aims to overcome the stereotyped dichotomy of woman protected/man protector,[17] a dichotomy that, it is best to remember, gives men the possibility of claiming such an unavoidable superiority as to justify their 'dominant position within the social order'.[18] However, according to this interpretation, it is not clear what benefits could come to women from their entrance into the armed forces, as long as they are excluded from combat roles – those very roles that at the same time exemplify and legitimize the position of 'protector'.

The second type of prescriptive analysis, instead, refers to the point of view of the military institution and, in parallel, to the supposed technical-objective necessities of war. The passage from compulsory conscription to voluntary service and the fall of birth rates would have persuaded military leaders of the convenience of opening the armed forces to women, in this way compensating for the lack of recruits. This type of measure should be taken with caution in order to respect the essential requisites of *efficiency* and *effectiveness* to which the military instrument must always primarily refer.[19]

Effectiveness would be negatively influenced by the entrance of women for two fundamental reasons: their greater physical weakness with respect to men and their disrupting effect on 'male bondings' – bondings that play such an important role in transforming a soldier into a valiant soldier and a crowd of people into a solid group of combatants.[20] As far as physical weakness is concerned, it must be stressed how, in today's panorama of war, the ever growing use of sophisticated arms and electronic devices have diminished the importance of force intended as brute force and reinforced, on the other hand, the necessity of having qualified personnel; for, despite the negative impact of female presence in wholly male groups, it has been noted that male bondings are not the only ties that favour the success of a group in combat and how the degree of their cohesion does not exclusively depend on factors tied to gender.[21]

With regard to efficiency, measured by the relationship between costs and benefits, in a situation of limited resources, the training of women soldiers instead of men seems to imply superior costs, deriving from the (usually) greater number of hours necessary for women to reach the same level of physical readiness as men; it is true, on the other hand, that the traditionally higher level of education of women entering the armed forces should reduce the duration of training that does not simply regard athletic fitness.

Therefore, the descriptive as well as the prescriptive approach (presented here in an extremely abbreviated form) cannot give converging answers to the question of whether women should or should not be part of the military institution.

A point of view that is generically defined as 'pacifist' or 'non-violent' is opposed to these approaches. It focuses its attention not so much on the objective necessities to which the access to military service by women would correspond or to the advantages that this would bring to them, as to the ideological and ethical choices that are conventionally associated with military service.

Rejecting, on principle, the use of force as a means of resolution of internal and international conflicts and considering the existing military system as the maximum expression of formalized violence, this approach condemns its existence and, then, contains within itself *a fortiori* a drastic refusal of any hypothesis of participation by women.

Between these two positions, the one that for convenience we will call the realistic and the pacifist one, dialogue is not 'ontologically' possible; this impossibility is often synthetically evoked by women writers that belong to the first category through the use of a sort of a ritual formula at the opening of their articles, in which they explain how they share and appreciate non-violent concerns, but how it is impossible to accept them as methodological premises if you intend to influence the reality and in order to be able to 'offer protection to innocent others'.[22] Alternatively, pacifism is dismissed as a disdainful refusal to 'mix with the dirt of daily external affairs', while hiding behind a 'moral superiority'.[23]

Is it possible to overcome the impasse that these observations impose on those interested in the debate 'women and armed forces'?

2. MILITARY SERVICE SEEN AS A PART OF THE WHOLE: THE SECURITY POLICY OF THE STATE AND THE CONSENSUS OF ITS CITIZENS

In order to do this it becomes necessary to go back a step and adopt a point of view that contains, as was mentioned in the opening, the double question of necessities and choices: it is the point of view of studies on security.

Within the framework of these studies, the value of the military institution is not considered principally in relation to the benefits that the citizens can get from the state (debate on citizenship), nor in relation to its efficiency and effectiveness (an aspect commonly studied by military tactics and strategy), but with primary reference to the very existence of the state and to its pursuit of security.

On one hand, the use of force between states, that is war, involves 'the reciprocal use of organized forces between two or more social groups, directed according to an overall plan or a series of plans for the achievement of a political object'.[24]

On the other, the state is defined, from Weber on, as the only institution capable of holding the legitimate monopoly of force, this becoming one of its fundamental components. This monopoly is exercised through the collection of means with which to wage wars (arms and men), conceptualizing the aims of national security and the responses to threats and, ultimately, by linking these two events (the collection of means to wage war and the conceptualization of security aims) in a functional way. In order to do this, reference must not be made solely to the technical and geopolitical necessities, but, and above all, to the values which a state pledges to support with regard to the citizens on which it imposes conscription (in countries where conscription exists) and with regard to the state against which it uses its armed forces.

In this perspective, recruitment becomes a fundamental device for the solution of national security problems and its study consequently cannot be separated from them. Recruitment is, thus, the means by which a state, through consensus, if we are considering a democratic state, gathers the necessary human resources to implement its monopoly of force.

The legitimacy of the use of force, based on the consensus of the citizens, depends on the capacity of the state to respond with a modicum of coherence and clarity to this complex set of problems. The public consensus that must be obtained in order to produce a credible military instrument must find its roots in two main fields: the one of values which the armed forces of a country pledge to support (in peacetime, this is reflected in the quality and the conditions of military life) and the one of the capacity of the armed forces to face the necessities of security of the state and of its citizens.

While war is 'a practical activity when once undertaken',[25] it is not the means of destruction which devastate, but men who, by using them, kill other men.[26] Then, everything that leads up to and follows war has a close relationship with ethical concerns, the definition of which everyone in a democratic system, independently of gender, is called to participate in. The importance of this concern must never be underestimated, not even in the case of a 'waged war', an event that cannot be reduced to a pure clash of forces in a field technically 'purified' of any human attribute.

The fact of being national, rational, socially organized and instrumental is then what distinguishes violence perpetrated by the state from the myriad of other forms that it can assume.[27]

The legitimacy of the use of force, which underwent a profound crisis, particularly in the United States during the years following the Vietnam War, for the very reason of its failing public consensus, has instead increased during the Gulf War. Why?

3. LEGITIMATION OF THE USE OF FORCE: THEORY AND EMPIRICAL EVIDENCE

It is difficult to pronounce unequivocally on the question of how and if a state can pursue political objectives by the use of force.

Empirical proof (such as responses to polls on the validity of the military option as a solution to the problem of the invasion by Iraq of Kuwait, participation in demonstrations and pacifist camps, opinion movements on the reform of the military system) often gives outcomes of difficult interpretation on the single question of the legitimacy of the use of force. It is clear, for example, that the rising number of requests for civilian service as an alternative to military service or that of suicides among conscripts in Italy at the end of the 1980s[28] cannot be interpreted on their own as signs of a global tendency contrary to the use of force, but stem from a wider group of causes.

The history of political doctrines, on the other hand, offers a variegated panorama of interpretations which also fail to lead to an unequivocal answer.

The theme of the aptitude of military means to serve political aims has always aroused the interest of political philosophers. Many theories have been elaborated that refer to four types of systems in the framework of which it is possible to analyse the phenomenon of war understood in the Clausewitzian way: *the socio-economic system, the internal political system, the international system and the system of values*. Reference to one system does not exclude, as we shall soon see, the simultaneous reference to another. Though being conscious of the inherent risk in any comparative effort that is abstracted from the historical condition in which a theory has been elaborated, it seems useful to review these theories briefly. This will be done not so much for evaluating their coherence, but to demonstrate the complexity of an argument too often described according to a political logic more than an intellectual one and to draw from its analysis an idea for orienting the pragmatic decision on whether women should enter the military system.

The *first group* of theories stresses the fact that the evolution of the socio-economic structures of a state influences the use of force in a decisive way. Wars are explained as being calculable effects of deep changes in the way society organizes its productive power.[29] A substantial part of the theories that originate from this basic concept (formalized in the first half of the nineteenth century by Comte following in the footsteps of Saint-Simon) stressed how the evolution of the socio-economic structure would have caused the disappearance of the phenomena of war because of its uneconomic nature within industrial societies whose strongholds (international exchange and commerce) were hit in a particularly negative way by the instability produced by conflicts. The incompatibility between war and industrial society was considered as being the very essence of this kind of society, which could not be defined, according to Comte, by a particular degree of development of the forces of production or by the use of advanced technologies, but rather by a substitution of war by work as the dominant activity and by the substitution of slavery by freedom.[30]

The Marxist theory, elaborated through successive phases of industrial development, in contrast to this optimistic point of view, stressed the essentially warlike nature of the capitalist economic system, which develops in two successive historical phases, one of imperialist wars of conquest and the other of wars between imperialistic states. The conflicts of the first phase are induced by the need to resolve the cyclical crisis of internal overproduction and to maintain competitiveness at an international level. To do this, new sources of raw materials are always needed (or cheap raw materials), new markets and particularly elevated levels of profit are constantly sought. This perpetual tendency of the capitalist state requires maintenance of a powerful military apparatus to safeguard the economic supremacy in its own spheres of influence; since the armed forces are ideal clients for private industries (being a guaranteed and solvent market) these in turn, thanks to intermingled interests based on economic profits, will try to induce the political decision-makers to create artificial arms markets, selling them off with loans and sales to allied states or with direct interventions in conflicts outside of national territory.[31]

The *second group* of theories emphasizes the ties between the nature of the political systems and the tendency of the governments that adopt them to resolve international controversies with military means. According to these authors, the historically undeniable belligerence of authoritarian regimes would depend on their nature and on their internal functioning mechanisms of power. Next to this observation one must stress the fact that even democracies (though historically not in conflict with one another, but against different political systems, considered hostile and dangerous) have demonstrated a high degree of belligerence. Howard, following in the footsteps of Montesquieu, has convincingly noted how the armed forces of democratic countries have fought, and continue to fight, with equal if not greater intensity than authoritarian nations, justifying their acts as being not so much a means of pursuing a national security goal but a means of pursuing a universal goal;[32] that is why both democracies and fanatical religious regimes agree on the legitimacy of 'just wars'. Above all, every democracy, through the use of mass conscription and propaganda demonizing the enemy, has contributed towards a globalization and radicalization of conflicts.[33]

The *third group* of theories refers to the nature of the international arena where the activity of a state is carried out. First of all, this arena cannot be considered as a system because it lacks any kind of a coercive mechanism that assures its members the right of existence – the way a state has – even if possessing a series of legal prescriptions on the behaviour of states. The international arena is consequently seen as anarchical, without any valid procedure for reconciling conflicting interests and in whose framework all the positive aspects of a given national political system can be jeopardized and destroyed by an external invasion. The violent nature of the international system is considered (from Thucydides on, through to Aron, up to Hoffman and Waltz) as the main source of legitimation for the maintenance of national armed forces. Though being susceptible to partial criticism – who, for example, is able to define where 'the best interests of international society lie'[34] and who guarantees that the preservation of the *status quo* at an international level is functional to the pursuit of a 'just' international order? – this conception has without a doubt been confirmed as being dominant in the postwar period. It in fact corresponds perfectly to the situation developed after the 1945 Yalta agreements, when the division of the world into two distinct spheres of influence and the possession of the atomic bomb by the two superpowers determined strong stability on the frontiers and the necessity of their constant intense defence for fear of leaving room to the 'hegemonic appetites' of the enemy. Bipolarity, tied to the nature of the new atomic weapons (the less Clausewitzian[35] or rather less flexible and adaptable to the variable national goals of a state[36]) acquired by the United States and the Soviet Union has favoured a durable stability in the European geopolitical field. The recent collapse of the bipolar system, moreover, together with the persistence of conventional conflicts, has legitimized the interpretation of the international arena as an anarchical system in which the states must have the military means to defend themselves from external aggression. Empirical proof of this has been furnished by the way in which Saddam Hussein put his hegemonic ambitions into action on Kuwait; the reaction of the international community (by means of war) has once again demonstrated the classical model of solution of controversies through the use of force.

The *last group* is not made up of a homogenous nucleus of theories, but is formed mostly of conceptions that refer to the sphere of ethic values as being explicative of the decline of the consensus in relation not so much to the use of force in modern societies as, and above all, to the armed forces *tout court*.

In this sense Hoffman recalled twenty years ago how the cultural revolution of the 1960s had inflicted a lethal blow to the concepts of discipline and acceptance of leadership.[37] These concepts are the very ones that characterize the armed forces, the way they have been traditionally considered up to now, and that principally have made the perpetuation of war possible – if what Rita Levi di Montalcini says is true, that the 'preferential' relationship between the male gender and war does not come from a genetic inclination of man (intended as male) to violence as much as from a cultural inclination to obedience that would permit his integration into the highly hierarchical military system.[38]

With regard to formative values, though, it is also true that the armed forces of Western countries have gone through a sort of revolution in the last twenty years. There are two ways to justify the gathering of human resources for military purposes on an ethical level. On one hand the system can have recourse to values such as 'duty', 'honour', 'the flag', 'civil solidarity' and consequently adopt recruitment based primarily on conscription; on the other hand, it can stress the importance of values such as rationality, efficiency, professionalism, economic welfare, and consequently adopt a system of voluntary recruitment. In some countries, the United States for example, the armed forces have undergone a development that has brought them, in the space of a few years, from one model to the other. What Moskos described in 1977 as the passage from an institutional model to an occupational one[39] has come about. This transformation has brought about a change in the qualifications of the subjects taking part in it: 'citizen soldiers' have become 'economic men'.[40]

While the ethos of 'duty' and 'honour' has lost credibility in the context of a war that more and more often relies on sophisticated technologies and on the 'invisibility' of the enemy, the ethos of efficiency and rationality has trouble finding a place in contemporary bureaucratic military apparatuses based on waste of non-productive resources.[41]

Therefore, as can be seen, the analysis of the internal characters of the state, be they socio-economic or political, leads to rather divergent conclusions with regard to the existing link between one of their variations (of internal characters) and the changes of trend in the legitimization of the use of force.

The analysis that refers to the main features of the international system, on the contrary, seems to lead to a straightforward conclusion: the use of force, under certain conditions, is legitimate and the state should be entrusted for that.

Finally, if we follow the last group of theories, they also seem to lead to a straightforward conclusion, but of an opposite sign: the diffusion of social criticism against a series of ethic values which have permeated the armed forces for centuries seems to point in the direction of a weakening of the legitimacy of the use of force.

4.   A PROVISIONAL CONCLUSION

While the state, in particular a medium power like Italy, finds itself acting in a pre-structured international context – it undergoes heavy conditioning and then has the tendency to mould the armed forces in reaction to a series of external 'necessities' – it still has the power of choosing which values to draw inspiration from, to structure such an armed force. From this point of view, the state must operate a 'choice' that cannot be disguised as an imposition: in fact it does not only derive from necessities of a technical or geopolitical nature, but also from ethical options that have to be explicit.

This is the main battlefield in which to gain the citizens' consensus towards an institution, the military, that has held and even now holds a fundamental role not only in the individual human experience of many citizens, but also in the relationship between states, in which this institution is 'spent' not only in the case of armed conflict – one need only think of the importance of the menace of the use of force in international diplomatic negotiations. The call cyclically advanced in Italy (the only country in NATO whose armed forces are completely masculine) in favour of the admittance of women to the military institution finds its primary justification in the attempt to resolve the problem of the consensus through a mechanism which, the clearer it is, the less convincing it becomes. Admittance on a voluntary basis in the armed forces is presented as an extra opportunity 'offered' to women on the road towards equality of rights and duties: in this manner an attempt is made to obtain an extension of public consensus towards an institution without suggesting solutions to its wrong-doings, but widening the very base of the participation in it.

This attempt is associated with politics devoted to creating 'a new image' of the army[42] that awkwardly mix the criteria of the traditional model with the 'economic' one, creating confusion instead of inspiring trust – with reference to this, one notices the different tones of the promotional campaigns launched by the Army within a year's distance from one another.[43]

The danger then is that women's consensus to the opening of the armed forces to them, intended abstractly as the acquisition of a right, turns the attention away from the true weaknesses of the armed forces and indirectly acts as a palliative to keep them alive as they are now. It is true that this opening could help to highlight the contradiction in which the armed forces find themselves; it is for this reason probably that, as Virgilio Ilari notes,[44] the debate on women soldiers has developed following a logic of political opportunities, legal 'pruderies', and scandalous curiosity of the media without ending up in any coherent policy in this field.

On the other hand, before supporting the hypothesis of opening the armed forces to women, it is necessary to question the nature of the institution they would be called to take part in and the nature of the political system of which this institution is the expression.

As far as Italy is concerned, the topic of the admittance of women into the armed forces is marginal compared to the central one that invests these two fields. There is above all, as was noted beforehand, a great confusion concerning the values the armed forces must promote: in contrast to erratic propaganda focusing on individualism and on the 'Rambo-like' characteristics of the applicants or, alternatively, on their 'protective' nature, lies the paralysing bureaucratic reality, which in Italy is not a prerogative of the armed forces alone. There also exists a diffused sense of inadequacy of the military instrument with regards to the tasks it is called to execute in an external field (in situations of *peacekeeping* as in those of armed assistance[45]) and in the internal one (assistance in the case of natural calamities, for example).

Last but not least, there is a profound lack of confidence of public opinion in the capacity of politicians to establish convincing security goals in the external field and to give efficient protection to the lives of Italy's citizens in the internal field, at least in a large part of the national territory.

A democratic state with a sufficiently defined national identity (that is, by simplifying to the maximum degree, without spectacular border troubles and without serious problems of ethnic cohabitation) – as is the case of Italy – can concentrate its attention towards 'internal' necessities of security rather than towards the external ones, defined as those situations that could endanger the very existence of the state as a territorial entity in itself (while the necessity of maintaining small contingents for *out of area* intervention with the principal goal of *peacekeeping* also exists).

Charles Tilly has expressed with great incisiveness the dilemma in which the critics of the European model of a national state as a dispenser of security find themselves:

Its obituary will be hard to write. On one side, we see the pacification of European civil life and the fashioning of more or less representative political institutions, both by-products of a state formation driven by the pursuit of military might. On the other side, we notice the rising destructiveness of war, the pervasive intervention of states in individual lives, the creation of incomparable instruments of class control. Destroy a state, and create a Lebanon. Fortify it, and create Korea. Until other forms displace the national state, neither alternative will do. The only real answer is to turn the immense power of national states away from war and toward the creation of justice, personal security, and democracy'.[46]

There are two possible roads to take: to concentrate attention towards internal security needs, opening the military institutions to society (an attempt was made in the 1960s with the so-called 'democratization' of the armed forces in Italy), reconsider its structure and expand its functions to wider sectors of national life. Or else, vice versa, limit its functions according to an ethic based on professionalism and rationality and thus not expand but on the contrary limit the tasks of its activities according to criteria of logic and economy (consider all the series of services that historically have no longer the motive of being militarized, from firemen to sanitary officials, and those managed by the military apparatus with inefficiency, arsenals for instance).[47]

The question of the admission of women to the armed forces can be correctly faced only after having given an answer to these problems.[48] Until this goal is reached, the most useful task that women can accomplish is that of contributing to the 'external control'[49] of the military apparatus for influencing or, at least, acquiring an even partial control of the decisions relating to the national security of the country. If one can say that a lot has been done in the field of information on the organization and regulations of the Italian armed forces, little has been obtained to make this 'theoretical' knowledge available outside the restricted circle of technically defined 'experts'; the military policy of the country has remained a 'restricted area'. At the same time one must hope that women will and will want to contribute to the solution of the problem of the 'reconversion' of the armed forces in terms of ethical values and internal goals. In the context of the analysis that has been employed up to now, it seems that this double function could be carried out with more incisiveness by many women outside of the military system rather than by a few inside.

Notes

1. It is the title of a paragraph of the volume by E. A. Cohen, *Citizens and Soldiers: The Dilemmas of Military Service* (Ithaca and London: Cornell University Press, 1985) pp. 25–41.

2. For the production of essays up to the 1980s reference is made to the bibliographical essay in N. L. Goldman (ed.) *Female Soldiers: Combatants or Noncombatants?* (Westport: Greenwood Press, 1982) pp. 291–5. A considerable increase of literature in this field has been registered in these last ten years, as can be seen from the bibliography presented at the end of this volume. Among all the contributions that have recently appeared, two worth noting that have already become classics in the memorialistic vein are: S. Saywell, *Women in War* (New York: Viking, 1985) and G. Braybon and P. Summerfield (eds), *Out of the Cage, Women's Experiences in Two World Wars* (London: Pandora, 1987); with regard to the female experience in the armed forces of the United States, Australia, Canada and Great Britain, see for example, D. Segal and W. Sinaiko (eds) *Life in the Rank and File: Enlisted Men and Women in the Armed Forces of USA, Australia, Canada and the United Kingdom* (Washington: Pergamon-Brasseys International Defense Publishers, 1985).

3. One must stress that some wartime chronicles are not concerned with experiences of support (direct or indirect) to the armed forces but with those 'suffered' by women as victims of war long before and much more than as collaborators of the armed forces; specifically for the Italian case see the book by M. Mafai, *Pane nero. Donne e vita quotidiana nella seconda guerra mondiale* (Milan: Mondadori, 1987). The emergence of this kind of war experience – which it is impossible to discuss here – is tied above all to the progressive erosion of the inviolability of the internal front. This inviolability, traditionally mined by guerrilla tactics, has suffered a concentrated attack since the First World War especially due to the development of bombing by aviation as a tactical means of support to terrestrial and maritime operations (First World War) and as a central support of the strategic offensive action against urban centres (Second World War).

4. A. Bravo, 'Introduzione', in A. Bravo (ed.) *Donne e uomini nelle guerre mondiali* (Rome-Bari: Laterza, 1991) p. xxi.

5. For all, see A. Marwick, *War and Social Change in the Twentieth Century* (London: Macmillan, 1974).

6. P. Summerfield, *Women Workers in the Second World War: Production and Patriarchy in Conflict* (London: Croom Helm, 1984); H. L. Smith (ed.) *War and Social Change: British Society in the Second World War* (Manchester University Press, 1986).

7. Bravo (ed.) *Donne e uomini nelle guerre mondiali*, p. xxiii.
8. M. R. Higonnet, 'Introduction', in W. R. Higonnet, J. Jenson, S. Michel and M. C. Weitz (eds) *Behind the Lines: Gender and the Two World Wars* (New Haven: Yale University Press, 1987) pp. 1–17; for an anthology of essays that adopt this more problematical point of view see A. Marwick (ed.) *Total War and Social Change* (New York: St Martin's Press, 1988).
9. J. Stiehm, 'The Effect of Myths about Military Women on the Waging of War', in E. Isaksson (ed.) *Women and the Military System* (London: Wheatsheaf, 1988) p. 104; see also N. Huston, 'The Matrix of War: Mothers and Heroes', in S. R. Suleiman (ed.) *The Female Body in Western Culture* (Cambridge Mass.: Harvard University Press, 1985) pp. 119–35.
10. C. Moskos, 'From Institution to Occupation', *Armed Forces and Society*, 1 (1977) pp. 41–50.
11. R. Kanter, *Men and Women of the Corporation* (New York: Basic Books, 1977).
12. K. Dunvin, 'Gender and Perceptions of the Job Environment in the US Air Force', *Armed Forces and Society*, 1 (1988) pp. 71–91, especially pp. 80–6.
13. L. B. De Fleur and R. L. Warner, 'Air Force Academy Graduates and Non-graduates: Attitudes and Self-Concepts', *Armed Forces and Society*, 4 (1987) pp. 517–33; C. L. Williams, *Gender Differences at Work: Women and Men in Nontraditional Occupations* (Berkeley: University of California Press, 1989).
14. J. Elshtain Bethke, *Women and War* (New York: Basic Books, 1987) pp. 49–56.
15. M. Janovitz, *Military Conflict* (Beverly Hills: Sage, 1975) pp. 77–8.
16. C. Enloe, *Ethnic Soldiers* (Athens: University of Georgia Press, 1980); also see her essay in the present volume.
17. J. H. Stiehm, 'The Protected, the Protector, the Defender', in *Women's Studies International Forum*, special issue on *Women and Men's Wars*, 3–4 (1982) p. 10; this refusal seems to have originated with the formulation of the question by Virginia Woolf, whose hostility to pacifism during the period preceding the Second World War was intimately tied to criticism with regard to the exclusion of women from military service (which made pacifism for women become a necessity rather than a choice). For Virginia Woolf this presumption did not come so much from the need to accede to the military system but rather from the need to found a society of women 'without a country' based on the refusal *a priori* of both war and peace, anchored to the strong call for universal citizenship, freed from particular obligations towards a state. V. Woolf, *Three Guineas* (New York: Harcourt Brace, 1938) p. 109; see also S. Gilbert, 'Soldier's Heart: Literary Men Literary Women, and the Great War', in Higonnet, Jenson, Michel, and Weitz (eds) *Behind the Lines*, pp. 220–1.
18. C. H. Enloe, *Does Khaki Become You?* (Boston: South End Press, 1983) p. 15.

19. For all of these, see two comments present in the already cited volume edited by Nancy Goldman and entirely dedicated to the argument: J. M. Tuten, 'The Argument against Female Combatants', pp. 237–65 and M. W. Segal, 'The Argument for Female Combatants', pp. 267–90.

20. The classical reference for this interpretation is L. Tiger, *Men in Groups* (New York: Random House, 1969) especially pp. 84–5.

21. M. C. Devilbiss, 'Gender Integration and Unit Deployment: A Study of GI Jo', *Armed Forces and Society*, 4 (1985) pp. 523–52, especially pp. 528–30.

22. See, for example, the beginning of the essay already quoted: Stiehm, 'The Protected, the Protector, the Defender', in Women's Studies International Forum, p. 367; by the same author, see also the 'Introduction' to J. H. Stiehm, *Arms and the Enlisted Woman* (Philadelphia: Temple University Press, 1989) especially pp. 1–4.

23. E. Goodman, article in the *Washington Post*, 1 November 1983; on the question of the debatable relationship between women, pacifism and military studies, see J. Elshtain Bethke and S. Tobias (eds) *Women, Militarism and the War: Essays in History, Politics and Social Theory* (Savage: Rowman and Littlefield, 1990).

24. M. Howard, 'Temperamenta Belli: Can War be Controlled?', in M. Howard (ed.) *Restraints on War* (Oxford: Oxford University Press, 1990) p. 1.

25. I. Clark, *Waging War: A Philosophical Introduction* (Oxford: Clarendon Press, 1990) p. 11.

26. C. Schmitt, *Theorie des Partisanen: Zwischenbemerkung zum Begriff des Politischen* (Berlin: Duncker & Humblot 1975).

27. Clark, *Waging War*, pp. 16–17; Howard, 'Temperamenta Belli', p. 1.

28. P. Bonetti, 'Il dibattito sulla condizione militare in un anno difficile', *Il Mulino*, 1 (1987) pp. 116–29.

29. W. B. Gallie, *Philosophers of Peace and War* (Cambridge: Cambridge University Press, 1978) p. 75.

30. See R. Aron, *La société industrielle et la guerre* (Paris: Plon, 1959) pp. 5–17; F. Ferrarotti, 'Introduzione', in F. Ferrarotti (ed.) *Comte. Antologia di scritti sociologici* (Bologna: Il Mulino, 1977) pp. 10–11.

31. See, for example, the chapter 'Absorption of Surplus: Militarism and Imperialism' in P. Baran and P. Sweezy, *Monopoly Capital* (Harmondsworth: Penguin, 1975) (1st edn 1966) pp. 178–214, and for a critical evaluation that has the merit of being clear and synthetic, Aron, *La société industrielle et la guerre*, pp. 30–9.

32. Howard, 'Temperamenta Belli', pp. 7–8.

33. S. Hoffman, 'The Acceptability of Military Force', *Adelphi Paper*, 102, *Force in Modern Societies: Its Place in International Politics* (London: ISS, 1973) p. 6.

34. Clark, *Waging War*, p. 23.

35. Hoffman, 'The Acceptability of Military Force', p. 7.

36. A defensive limited nuclear war would have unimaginable consequences not only on the territory where it is fought, but on the world's ecosystem.

37. Hoffman, 'The Acceptability of Military Force', pp. 2–13.
38. Cit. in U. Capuzzo, 'Tra focolare e campo di Marte: la donna nella realtà militare dei tempi', *Rivista Militare*, 6 (1982) p. 2; the observations on aggressiveness done on groups of chimpanzees by Frans de Waal tend to demonstrate the biological rather than cultural character of the inclination of male chimpanzees to the vertical hierarchical form (that presumes an inclination to obedience); F. de Waal, *Sex Differences in the Stability of Friendship and Rivalries among Chimpanzees*, talk given at the X ISRA convention (International Society for Research on Aggression) Siena, 6–12 November 1992.
39. Moskos, 'From Institution to Occupation'.
40. C. Moskos, 'The American Enlisted Man in the All-Volunteer Army', in D. Segal and W. Sinaiko (eds) *Life in the Rank and File* (Washington: Pergamon–Brassey's, 1985); also see the essay by Elisabetta Addis in this volume.
41. Hoffman, 'The Acceptability of Military Force', pp. 2–13.
42. We cannot take into consideration, here and now, the advertising policies of the three armed forces, which vary considerably and would necessitate a separate essay. The Army has been chosen because it exemplifies the general discussion, but does not reflect the 'general' policy of the armed forces.
43. The first publicity campaign launched after the end of the Gulf War depicted a tank driver scrutinizing the desolate surrounding desert from the turret of his tank, illuminated by a pale red sun. The enigmatic caption said: 'Italian Army. New Force. Armed. Are you ready to take it seriously?' And again: 'If you're not afraid to put yourself to the test, to train hard, to face situations at their limits, today your place is in the army. But be careful the mission is difficult.' Commenting on the advertisement, Ferdinando Camon wrote that the soldier to whom the advertisement refers to was 'not the son of Garibaldi and the Constitution, but of Frederich Nietzsche and his Power of the Will'; *La Stampa*, 26 Feb. 1991. To the comment by Camon must be added the more material one on the plausibility of the situation presented by the publicity: it is in fact well known that the army was not part of the contingent sent by Italy to the Gulf. The quality of advertising campaigns by the Italian Army has subsequently been changing (February–March 1992) and gave rise to publicity for the course of sub-lieutenant of the military academy of Modena which showed an Italian soldier busy guarding a refugee camp – presumably Kurdish. The caption that accompanied the advertisement was the following 'We're looking for strong officers for a world that respects the weak.' It's significant that the old caption 'Italian Army. New force. Armed. Are you ready to take it seriously?' has evolved into the much more calibrated: 'Army, New Force. Armed' (sweetened from national and superman-like features). The army now has only to choose which of the two images it intends to propose as definitive.
44. See his essay in this volume.

45.   One must acknowledge the fact that the Italian armed forces have been engaged with positive results, in the last ten years, in various operations of peacekeeping.

46.   C. Tilly, *Coercion, Capital, and European States, AD 990–1990* (Cambridge: Basil Blackwell, 1990) p. 225.

47.   On these topics, see the interventions collected in the chapter 'In cerca di alternative', in the volume L. Menapace and C. Ingrao (eds) *Né in difesa né indivisa* (Rome: Gruppo misto sinistra indipendente Regione Lazio, 1988) pp. 109–33 (the volume contains the talks given at a convention organized in 1987 by the 'Coordinamento donne elette nelle liste del PCI' from Lazio and 'Coordinamento donne Fuori la guerra dalla storia').

48.   The proposal made by Minister of Defence Andò at the end 1992 – regarding a global re-organization of military service and within this re-organization, the opening of the service to women on a voluntary basis – is, from a formal point of view, an important step in the direction of 'contextuality'.

49.   See G. Pasquino, *Elementi per un controllo politico sulle forze armate* (Bologna: Il Mulino, 1975).

3 The Constitution of a Gendered Enemy

Valeria E. Russo

Who was Penthesilea? Clearly, I have not done justice
to her, nor she to me. With her piercing eyes and
cutting tongue, for me she was a little too sharp.
Every appearance, every phrase of hers was a challenge
to someone or other.... The inhabited world, as far
as we knew it, had revolted against us, with ever more
cruelty, ever more fervour. Against us women, said
Penthesilea. Against us humans, retorted Arisbe.
Penthesilea: The men will be satisfied. Arisbe: You
call them satisfied at reducing themselves to butchers?
Penthesilea: They are butchers. They are just doing
what turns them on. Arisbe: And us? What if we became
butchers too? Penthesilea: We do what has to be done.
But it does not amuse us. Arisbe: Ought we to do what
they do in order to demonstrate our difference?
Penthesilea: Yes. Aeno: But that's no way to live.
Penthesilea: Not to live. But to die, yes.... I rebuked
Penthesilea fiercely: You want to die, so you make the
others keep you company.... Cheek!, shrieked
Penthesilea. And you are the one to say that! You,
are neither fish nor flesh! A little more and we'd have
been tooth and nail at each other.... Until now, I had
forgotten all that.

(Author's translation from the German: Christa Wolf,
Kassandra (Hamburg: Lutherhand, 1992, 13th edn))

1. GENDER AND POWER

Gender is being taken up as an analytical category towards
the end of the twentieth century. In a famous 1986 article,

the American historian Joan W. Scott defined it as a mode of referring to the social organization of the relation between the sexes, a notion introduced in order to 'discover the range in sex roles and in sexual symbolism in different societies and periods, to find what meanings they had and how they functioned to maintain the social order or to promote its change'.[1] Often the term 'gender' has been used to refer to the areas (whether structural or ideological) that concern women, children and the family, while areas like diplomacy, international relations, high politics and war have not yet been explicitly tested against the touchstone of the relation between the sexes: men, understood as 'public men' (J. Elshtain Bethke), seem in fact to exist 'beyond gender relations to the same degree they dominate them. While the imperative that women's history always be related to men's has become commonplace, up to now the reverse has hardly been true. Military history and the history of warfare are a case in point. They have dealt exclusively with men – and for good reason, since in the Western world (at least within Europe) war has generally been a form of direct confrontation between groups of men. Nonetheless, explicitly male-specific issues have not been raised in this field, for example in its connection with the history of masculinity'.[2]

It is important to stress that, as a constitutive feature of the social relations gender is a primary mode of signifying *power relationships*. Changes in social organization are always reflected in the changes that come about in the representation of power, and are marked at symbolic level starting from a reference to being male and being female, to the masculine and the feminine. As has been noted by Joan W. Scott, it need not surprise one that the power relationships among nations and their status as colonial subjects have in turn been expressed and legitimated in terms of relations between men and women:

> The legitimizing of war – of expending young lives to protect the state – has variously taken the forms of explicit appeals to manhood (to the need to defend otherwise vulnerable women and children), of implicit reliance on belief in the duty of sons to serve their leaders or their

(father) the king and of associations between masculinity and national strength...; the binary opposition and the social process of gender relationships both become part of the meaning of power itself; to question or to alter any aspect threatens the entire system.[3]

2. GENDER AND WAR

In recent decades a growing number of publications have dealt with the question of gender and war: the bibliography annexed to this volume may give an initial idea of the breadth of the topics covered in sometimes highly differentiated disciplinary areas. One of the results of this research concerns the questioning of man as 'just warrior' in stereotypic opposition to the image of woman as 'beautiful soul' on the level of symbolic relationships: I shall confine myself to referring by way of example to the analysis done in this connection by Jean Elshtain Bethke in her volume on *Women and War*, where she challenges this dichotomy on the basis of a broad range of material on the Second World War, and on the American Civil War, using references to personal memoirs, political theory, literature and the cinema.[4] Manifestly, the image of woman as the bearer *par excellence* of values of peace (how can she who generates life wish to contribute to creating death?) is historically justified by the front-rank role women have had within pacifist movements in this century: suffice it to mention the mobilization of masses of women in the demonstrations surrounding the two world wars. For this image – reassuring in many ways to both men and women – is nonetheless called in question at the point when armed conflicts cease to be 'men's business', but start to take the shape of aspects of the public sphere that emerge in places where the 'sexual contract' (Pateman) is violated and into which the female presence actively erupts, a presence which – in frequently disquieting and contradictory fashion – is also the object of the egalitarianism demanded by the contemporary emancipationist and feminist movements.

3. MALE ENEMY VERSUS FEMALE ENEMY

The participation of women in contemporary armed conflicts raises the question of the shape the image of the enemy is to take on in a situation in which (in Clausewitzian terms) 'politics is continued by other means'.[5] What may be the symbolic twists to which this image will be subject?

But what is the *enemy*? Perhaps, to a first approximation, one may start from the classical definition given of it in contemporary thought by Carl Schmitt in his famous essay on 'The concept of the "political"':

> The enemy is not the competitor or adversary in general. Nor is the enemy the private adversary that hates us on the basis of feelings of antipathy. The enemy is only a body of *men* [my emphasis] fighting at least virtually, that is on the basis of a real possibility, and opposing another human group of the same type. The enemy is only the public enemy, since everything that has to do with a grouping of this nature ... ipso facto becomes public. The enemy is the hostis, not the inimicus in the broader sense...; there is no need to hate the enemy in the political sense personally, and it is only in the private sphere that any meaning can be attached to loving one's enemy, that is, one's own adversary ... The concept of friend and enemy involves the possibility, in real terms, of a fight. This term is employed, glossing over all the casual or contingent changes brought by historical development in military technique and in weapons ... The concepts of friend, enemy and fighting take on their real significance from the fact that they refer specifically to the real possibility of physical killing ... War is only the extreme realization of hostility. It has no need to be something everyday and normal, nor to be seen as something ideal or desirable: it must, however, exist as a real possibility in order for the concept of enemy to be able to retain its meaning.[6]

I have cited this article at such length because the preconditions for attaining the status of hostis are paradigmatically associated at every point with the male gender: the enemy *fights*, is *public*, *flees from feeling*, and, not least, is the *citizen who kills*. This definition does not leave any room for a female enemy. History certainly offers figures of fighting women, the 'Dread Few': think of some of the female figures in Boccaccio's *De mulieribus claris* (a text that may, by the way, be regarded as one of the virtual precursor of 'women's history'), for instance Triaria: 'donna di estrema ferocia' (ob adversum mulieribus morem), she fights boldly alongside her husband Aulus Vitellius (brother of Lucius) and Vespasian. In a surprise night attack on Terracina, a city ruled by the Volsci and besieged by Vespasian's troops, Triaria shows how far her fighting ability goes:

> Resolved to conquer for her husband, armed with the sword in the midst of Vitellius's soldiers, she flung herself, now here now there, on those unfortunates, in the darkness of night, as they stumbled in total confusion and the darts rained down amid blood and the groans of the dying. It is told that when the city was reconquered she, following the iron law of war, was pitilessly cruel with the enemy, with extreme ferocity.[7]

But Triaria, like other figures of women warriors who historically existed, was obeying the law of the father; it was alongside the men that she was defending the law of her father and of the city. [8] But it is in myth that Western culture elaborates the figure of the irreducible female enemy, in which woman is war. I am here referring, of course, to the powerful mythic figure of the Amazon.

4. THE POWER OF MYTH

Myths should be regarded not as distorted answers to well-posed problems, but as narrative procedures, 'meaningful-nesses' freely produced, that engender problems. In Hans Blumenberg's words: 'What underlies the appeal of the mythic configurations is not the persuasiveness of ancient answers to presumed eternal enigmas of humanity, but the implicit nature of the questions disclosed, identified and articulated in the process of the assimilation of myths and the elaboration to which this subjects them'.[9]

Interrogating the myth also means, however, representing what is not, what is not current, what has been absorbed and cancelled, through a work of focusing that enables us to 'select', to 'steal' from the myth itself, while bearing in mind that for the two genders things work in different ways: for men, there exists a 'theatre of images in which it is their subjectivity that is called on to recognize itself', while for women 'there is the same theatre, imposed by a male subject, in which they are not the subject, but the object, of others' thought': the symbolic order in which both are inserted is, as we know, that of the patriarchal order.[10]

5. ORIGIN OF THE MYTH OF THE AMAZONS

The first traces of the myth date back to the 8th century BC in Greece, at the start of the archaic period. The first point to note is the extremely uncertain etymology of the term 'Amazon': the variety of etymological interpretations has itself proliferated a large number of versions of the myth, sometimes very far from each other.

Here are some:

1. From the Greek prefix '*a*' and '*mazos*', signifying 'de' and 'breasts' or 'debreasted women'.
2. From the Greek augmentative prefix '*a*' and '*mazos*' signifying 'big-breasted'.
3. From '*Masa*' (moon), or 'priestess of the Moon' (Caucasus).
4. From '*ha-mazan*' (warrior)/'*hain-aza*' (battle) – phonologically related to Greek '*mach-*'(fight) (Iran).

Homer calls them *antiàneirai*, that is, the antithesis of the hero: as strong as men, so much so as to be able to fight them, and hostile to men; they are represented as women warriors on horseback, in short tunic or multi-coloured trousers, with one shoulder bare and armed with a bow or doubleaxe, like the Scythians. Four celebrated Greek demigods, Heracles, Bellerophon, Achilles and Theseus, and also the young Priam when Prince of Troy, fought them. They were *par excellence androktònoi*, murderesses, or more exactly man-killers. Their specific peculiarity is to live in communities where the laws assign all military functions to their sex, with the baser tasks (forging their arms) and slavery being reserved to men, not to mention the fact that male children are mutilated at birth, an arm or leg being broken to make them incapable of war. The females have one breast burnt off, the right one, to prevent the protuberance interfering with the bow shots. The theses of such as Bachofen on the actual historical existence of the Amazons are unlikely to find many supporters today, despite their undoubted fascination (Bachofen firmly believed that

> We have before us not fictions, but lived fates. The Amazons and Bellerophon rest on a real foundation, not a poetic one. They are experiences of the mortal race, expressions of fates that were really experienced ... Amazonism is but one form of gynaecocracy ... and the fight against the Amazons corresponds to the rise of the paternal principle. The lunar, Amazonic principle is annihilated by the powers of light.[11]

It should however be noted how the myth of the Amazons, handed down from antiquity and found on three continents, expresses as few others do the 'poetry and terror', the fear and fascination, of 'female power': when woman seizes power – and for male culture armed power represents the most unequivocal expression of power! – the result is not just negation of the basic prerequisites of the 'polis', but the persecution of the male sex and the degradation of the human race itself. Woman becomes dangerous and awesome as being armed, but also as being sexually potent, not subject to control of reproductive choices. Gynaecophobia is expressed in this myth specifically through terror of the woman's body, of the sexual difference. It is told that the Amazons cut or burnt a breast (or both) for practical reasons: but the Scythian simple bow, for instance, obviates this necessity. Moreover, they are always depicted with both breasts, or a breast bare; but this amputation cuts into the female body the visible mark of the *bad woman* and the *bad mother.*[12]

As has been noted, the Amazon myth recurs and goes through intense moments of romanticization whenever there is a need to rewrite and requestion the symbols underlying it:

this comes about when two phenomena occur together: the outside political and military threat represented by the 'barbarians' and the internal threat represented by a change to the code governing the relations between the sexes .... An enemy may defeat and exterminate a nation, but it is not always seen as a generic danger to humanity as a whole. It is only when there is concommitant manifestation of the war between the sexes, when the roles allegedly guaranteed by the gods, on which social coexistence is based, are called in question again, that male culture feels threatened and a need is perceived to redefine the limits and the competences between the sexes, to rewrite, in the name of pacification, the laws of male rule and female submission. It is then that it becomes necessary to circulate symbols and models that make the danger explicit and make the new order not just acceptable, but attractive enough to induce the social subjects to spontaneously take it as their norm.[13]

6.   FEMINISM AND THE AMAZON MYTH

From the 1970s onwards, European and North American feminists have repeatedly discussed this mythological heritage, giving it a variety of interpretations (coming notably from the more intransigent element of radical feminism).[14]

It is interesting to note that one of the areas where resemanticization of the Amazon myth has given less expected outcomes has been the science fiction of a North American stamp: science fiction as 'mythology of the modern world' (Ursula K. Le Guin), and women's science fiction, in particular, has sought to free the Amazon from the stereotype of the Amazon: often the 'heroines' Amazonness' has been a means of highlighting their independence (in this connection see such authors as Marion Zimmer Bradley, Susan McKee Charnas, Joanna Russ).[15]

It should finally be pointed out how, in the search for 'female genealogies' not all women's culture has agreed to recognize these mother warriors, 'no longer imperfect' citizens to be sure, who nonetheless require a reappraisal to the roots of armed violence, and a confrontation with the link between woman and the warrior role. Today, I feel, the feminine, taking its place between power and potency, can now start to tackle that repression (*Verdrängung*).

Notes

1. J. Scott, 'Gender: A Useful Category of Historical Analysis', *American Historical Review*, 91 (1986) p. 105. See also N. Zemon Davis, 'Women's History in Transition: the European Case', *Feminist Studies*, 3 (1975–6), p. 90.

2. G. Bock, 'Women's History and Gender History: Aspects of An International Debate', *Gender & History*, (1989) p. 17. On the dichotomy private/public see J. Elshtain Bethke, *Public Man, Private Women* (Princeton University Press, 1981).

3. Scott, 'Gender: A Useful Category of Historical Analysis', p. 107.

4. J. Elshtain Bethke, *Women and War* (New York: Basic Books, 1987).

5. One of the classical works on strategies and conflicts between populations and nations is a book which has come to us thanks to a woman: I refer to *Vom Kriege* (On War) by Karl von Clausewitz, which was edited by his wife Maria after he died. In the 1832 preface to this over 700-page volume she wrote as follows: 'You are completely right if you find it strange that a female hand should dare to accompany a work on war subjects with a preface; [...nonetheless] I am sure that there will be no doubts on the nature of the feeling which enabled me to overcome the shyness that always makes it difficult for women to appear in public, even playing a secondary role'.

6. C. Schmitt, *The Concept of Political* (Rutgers: Rutgers University Press, 1976).

7. G. Boccaccio, *De mulieribus claris*, in *Tutte le opere*, vol. X, edited by V. Zaccaria (Milan: Mondadori, 1987) p. 391.

8. On the figure of the woman warrior, see for exemple chapters IX and X of the volume of P. Samuel, *Amazones, guerrieres et gaillardes* (Brussels: Edition Complexe, 1975) pp. 185-238. On the figure of the queen warrior see A. Fraser, *Bodicea's Chariot. The Warrior Queens* (London: Weidenfeld and Nicolson, 1988).

9. H. Blumenberg, 'Wirklichkeitbegriff und Wirkungspotential des Mythos', in M. Fuhrmann (ed.) *Terror und Spiel. Probleme des Mythosrezeption* (Munich: Wilhelm Fink Verlag, 1971) p. 34.

10. A. Cavarero, *Nonostante Platone* (Rome: Editori Riuniti, 1990) p. 4.

11. J. J. Bachhofen, *Il matriarcato* (1861) I (Turin: Einaudi, 1988) pp. 95, 99. For a reconstruction of the Amazonic myth see G. Cadogan Rothery, *The Amazons in Antiquity and Modern Times* (London: F. Griffiths, 1910); see also D. von Bothmer, *Amazons in Greek Art* (Oxford: Clarendon, 1957); Sir Gahalad (pseud. of Bertha Eckstein-

Diener), *Mütter und Amazonen. Liebe und Macht im Frauenreich* (1932) (Berlin/Frankfurt: 1987); M. Hammes, *Die Amazonen. Vom Mutterrecht und der Erfindung des gebärden Mannes* (Frankfurt: 1982).

12.   W. Lederer in *Gynecofobia ou la peur des femmes* (Paris: Payot, 1970) p. 57 underlined that Amazons have been considered 'des étrangères belliqueuses, que les héros grecs finirent par vaincre et que l'opinion antique considérait avec un mélange d'effroi, d'estime et de pitié'.

13.   M. Meiorin, 'Amazzoni dal mito al fumetto', in *Donne e guerra. Mito e storia* (Udine: DARS, 1989) p. 24.

14.   For instance, Uta Treder has recently underlined that the myth as such became one of the key subjects of the *Frauenforschung* in Germany 'androgeny became very soon a crucial issue of this debate, a kind of line of division as well' (U. Treder, *Il mito dell'androgino nella letteratura romantica*, in R. Svandrlik (ed.) *Ondina e le altre* (Rome: 1992). Extremely interesting remarks on the Amazonic myth are to be found in Christa Wolf's novel *Cassandra* (1983).

15.   See M. Zimmer Bradley, *The Shattered Chain* (New York: DAW, 1976); S. McKee Charnas, *Motherlines* (New York/Berkeley: 1976); J. Russ, *The Female Man* (New York: 1975) and J. Russ, 'When it Changed' in H. Ellison (ed.), *Again, Dangerous Visions* (New York: Doubleday, 1972). See also J. A. Salmonson (ed.) the two anthologies *Amazons!* (New York: DAW, 1979) and *Amazons II* (New York: DAW, 1982).

4 An Overview of Stressors in the Careers of US Servicewomen
Patricia B. Hanna

In 1973 the United States shifted to an all-volunteer military as a result of a declining male manpower pool between the ages of 17 and 21 and widespread anti-draft public sentiment in the aftermath of the Vietnam War.[1] Since that time the number of servicewomen has risen from less than 1 per cent of the services to approximately 11 per cent.[2] More than 228,000 women now serve in the US armed forces.

Judging from their personal accounts, a whole host of questions still remain about assignments that build careers, equal opportunities for promotion, combat service and over-all acceptance. The aim of this paper is to describe the stressors encountered by women in the US armed forces today.

The difficulties met with by servicewomen can be best sensed by allowing the women to speak for themselves. This mid-level Navy lieutenant commander with 12 years of experience had the following comments:

> In the past two years I've had my boss make a pass at me; I've been directly lied to by members of the headquarters staff; I've been accused of lying to members of this same staff and it has been rumored that I'm carrying on an illicit affair with one of my subordinates. My counterparts (all male) are publicly lauded and held up for emulation while I'm publicly criticized. On more than one occasion the staff has neglected to fill me in on vital information, then has badmouthed me for not knowing what's going on. This job should have been my stepping stone to commander – it's more than likely to be a brick wall. I am

frustrated, angry, stressed out and beginning to dread coming to work. I'm close to throwing in the towel. It's hard to keep a good attitude when I know that almost whatever I do is going to be wrong or inadequate or not quite enough.

Just because you're paranoid doesn't mean they're not really out to get you.[3]

These comments address many of the issues that are cited in the literature as being primary stressors. Sexual harassment, boundary heightening, fraternization regulations, double work standards for men and women and advancement difficulties are some of the more conspicuous stressors that servicewomen are confronted with.

When describing the military environment, many servicewomen, like the one quoted previously, mention problems of acceptance. Marine Brigadier General Gail Reals was quoted as saying upon her retirement last year: 'There is still a very basic issue of acceptance. We talk about sexual harassment, we talk about all these things, but to me they're all symptoms. To me the illness is basic acceptance'.[4] This basic problem of acceptance renders itself as stress in the military environment in many forms.

1.   COMBAT EXCLUSION[5]

Possibly the most highly visible and often cited example of lack of acceptance on an organizational level is servicewomen's occupational segregation. Although women receive equal compensation for equal work, they are barred from as many as 50 per cent of all occupational specialities because of combat exclusion rules.[6] The consequences of excluding women from combat-linked occupations are (1) loss of economic opportunity: and (2) obstacles to career advancement. Both result in psychological pressure not experienced by servicemen.

First, women lose out on economic rewards. For example, the Army College Fund pays servicemen and women up to $14,000 in addition to GI-Bill payments (a kind of educational scholarship programme for veterans) if they enlist for four years in 'critical skill' areas, which are mainly in combat units. The bonus programmes provide rewards for enlistment or re-enlistment in selected career fields (again, mainly the combat units) with cash payments of up to $8,000.

Second, servicewomen are denied access to a good number of significant career fields which would allow them to accumulate the kind of military experience sought by promotion boards. It is common knowledge that men who serve in combat career fields receive promotions faster than those in support or administrative careers. A recent Defense Department study of promotion policies found that 84 per cent of 25,000 female officers held the lowest three ranks, compared with 64 per cent for the same number of males.[7]

Moreover, the combat exclusion policy negatively affects the decisions women make about re-enlistment. Last year, the Air Force's retention rate for female pilots was 30 per cent, compared with 43 per cent for male pilots.[8] In general, women have tended to remain in the military for shorter periods than men.[9]

The absence of opportunity for growth in one's job is an important source of stress. In a recent study on the psychological well-being of Caucasian women, Baruch, Barnett and Rivers found that dull and dead-end jobs were strongly associated with diminished feelings of well-being.[10] Because servicewomen are unable to advance at the same rate as men, they may tend to undervalue their own achievements relative to those of men, developing self-images which reflect their situations.

Another psychological effect of combat exclusion is a decrease in expectations which may also result in a loss of interest in quality of performance. As observed by Kanter in *Men and Women of the Corporation*,[11] individual expectations increase when people have good jobs with advancement opportunity. Further, workers in positions with little power or career advancement opportunity will not succeed as much as persons who have growth-oriented jobs with associated power.[12] Diminished self-esteem and decreased expectations resulting from lack of equal advancement opportunity are likely to provide little incentive for top performance, thus reinforcing traditional sex stereotypes of women as being less capable than men. Combat exclusion may affect the way that servicewomen perform and are thus viewed and treated by their male colleagues.

2. ATTITUDES TOWARDS SERVICEWOMEN IN ORGANIZATIONAL CULTURE

Organizational settings may in some ways be microcosms of the culture in which they are found, but it is observed by Kanter in *Men and Women of the Corporation* that the dominant group defines the culture of an organization.[13] Taking into account that nearly a full 90 per cent of military service personnel are male, it follows that masculine norms and values are reflected by the organization's culture. Furthermore, young men who enter military training tend to be more politically conservative and conventional in their attitudes toward the social order as compared with their non-military peers.[14] As a result, the dominant norms and values of the military organization are not only masculine, but are on the conservative/conventional end of the continuum of masculine norms and values.

What does this have to say about the attitudes of servicemen towards females who have chosen non-traditional employment (defined as those jobs in which 75 per cent or more of those employed are men)[15] such as military service? In a study done by Duncan and Duncan in 1978 it was found that only 33 per cent of the sample (a cross-section of male and female US citizens) responded positively to the idea that there are no types of work that women should not do.[16] Research indicates that women violating sex-role expectations in job selection are awarded less social standing and judged less likeable than those conforming to such expectations.[17]

If we agree that servicemen tend to subscribe to more conventional social norms, it is likely that the military environment is one in which women frequently encounter unaccepting attitudes. Addressing this issue one woman marine commented:

Being a woman marine is really hard. Your male counter-parts aren't always as accepting on a professional level as you'd want them to be. It's an undertone, it's an attitude. When you mess up...they will say 'Well, that's because she's a woman.' It throws something in your face that you never even suspected was there.[18]

Servicemen behave at times as if traditional sex-role stereo-types were accurate, for example, by assuming that women are relatively dependent, passive, gentle, warm and would not make as effective, 'strong' leaders as would men. It has been suggested that one effect of the traditional cultural expectation that women behave deferentially is to create conflict with their feelings of confidence as leaders and their willingness to take responsibility, and may also result in mixed feedback when they do.[19] When male managers hold expectations of female behaviour based on traditional stereo-types, difficulties in supervision may occur. This may be ex-perienced by women as failure by supervisors to give them support.

Enlisted men and officers who have lived in a male-domin-ated military world all of their lives sometimes admit that it has been difficult to adjust to having females around. In a recent study it was found that the most positive male atti-tudes prior to the first-time integration of females on a ship occurred where the captain, who had requested command of a vessel with a mixed crew, had prepared with care and pride for the reception of women sailors.[20]

The findings of one recent study indicated that most servicewomen are convinced that luck determines whether they will be supported or discriminated against by those in command.[21] Even though there are many 'unknowns' ac-companying any new job, men are usually able to expect that they will progress beyond initiation into acceptance and in-tegration. For women there are no guarantees.

3. BOUNDARY HEIGHTENING

The literature on gender studies in the workplace cites another kind of behaviour – boundary heightening – as likely to be found in organizations which are dominated by members of one sex and include token members of another sex. Boundary heightening includes behaviours by dominant group members which emphasize their similarities and contrast or exaggerate the differences of token members in order to exclude them. These behaviours occur in varying degrees, from uneasiness of dominant members when minorities are present, to overt actions by dominant members to exaggerate their commonality and the minorities' differences.[22] A graphic example of boundary heightening can be seen in the following quotation from a letter to the editor of the *Navy Times* written by a male officer regarding the issue of women in combat.

> Warriors kill. If someone cannot kill, regardless of the reason(s), that individual is not a warrior. Men make the best warriors in comparison to women because men are better at killing in war.
>
> Women cannot compete on a battlefield as they cannot compete in professional sports against men. Women do not hold even one olympic world record for strength or speed. Women are weaker and slower on average as well. Strength, not weakness, wins battles and wars.
>
> Add to these undeniable physiological facts and the effects of socialization of women in American society and a simple fact becomes clearly evident to all but the most confused and misguided – women are no better suited to win wars than men are suited to have babies.
>
> In peace, women posing as America's warriors are annoying. In war, women posing as America's warriors could lead only to dishonorable defeat.
>
> Women who claim the title soldier, sailor, airman or marine bring to mind an old saying – 'you can paint black stripes on a white horse and call it a zebra, but that doesn't make it one'.[23]

These attitudes are stressful to servicewomen by assaulting their self-esteem and making them feel isolated and unaccepted.

Servicewomen also exhibit boundary heightening behaviours in settings where they are found in groups of relatively large numbers. A humorous example of these kinds of behaviours by women can be seen in the following quotation taken from an interview with servicewomen during the Gulf War. A female Air Force captain had this to say to explain the large female presence in the desert, despite official Pentagon protests that servicewomen were not being deployed to the front lines:

> U.S. Defense Secretary Dick Cheney was going to send over five thousand more Marines to reinforce the desert front lines, but he decided to send over five hundred women with premenstrual stress instead. Cheney rightly figured the women would retain water better and shoot anything that moved.[24]

Servicewomen use this and other kinds of humour to accentuate their differences from their male colleagues. This is one way they cope with the pressures of being token members of a predominantly male group.

4.   SOCIAL ISOLATION

Not only must a woman endure the stress of being socially isolated when she happens to be the only woman assigned to a particular work unit, but boundary heightening behaviours on the part of servicemen can, in effect, deny her access to any social relationships. One Navy officer, in a second tour where she was still the lone woman commented:

> During my first tour...I was very alone. Being on a ship is hard because it's a truly male environment. A group of talking, laughing men would become silent as I approached. My presence continually infringed on their inalienable right to be men. To feel at all times like a guest was very unpleasant.[25]

Such total isolation over long periods of time is not the habitual case. However, the stress experienced by servicewomen who must become accustomed to systematic exclusion should not be underrated.

For female officers, the effects of social isolation may be double. In settings where there are few women, the expectation on the part of enlisted servicewomen may be that female officers behave first as a part of the women's contingent, and second as officers. These expectations may be subtly expressed and can create stress for female officers who may be lonely and want to be friendly, but whose difference in rank dictates that their first responsibility is as an officer. As we shall see later, military rulings prohibit any appearance of favouritism.

Women are inclined to be more relationship-oriented than are men.[26] One coping mechanism that servicewomen use to their advantage to deal with stress is to seek socialization with their female peers. Being cut off from the support of other women for long periods of time may be one of the most difficult stressors that servicewomen are forced to cope with. However, when they do find a supportive, accepting, primarily male work unit, they talk about becoming 'one of the guys' or 'buddies' with their male colleagues. These relationships seem to form the same kind of supportive friendship group that women have had traditionally with other women and can serve as a buffer against stress.

5.   DOUBLE STANDARDS

Another pressure that tends to be exerted on military women is that unrealistically high performance standards are set for them. Kanter has proposed that the female token-group member does not have to work hard to have her presence noticed, but she does have to work hard to have her achievements noticed.[27] In the more traditionally masculine Military Occupational Specialties (MOSs), women find themselves in a contradictory position. In order to be considered capable, they work harder than men. However, if they earn special consideration because of outstanding performance, they are suspected of having benefited from favouritism.

Conditions have improved for women in today's military, although the existence of a double standard is still referred to quite regularly. A female Army sergeant was quoted as saying, 'A guy can screw up and no one says a word, but let a woman make just one mistake – watch out!'.[28] In a 1985 study it was reported that performance pressures and a lack of command support for women's presence on ships contributed to dissatisfaction.[29] Furthermore, in a survey of the first year of female cadets' integration at Annapolis, the Navy's prestigious officer-training academy, approximately one-half of women respondents reported stress resulting from the need to prove themselves, and one-third admitted experiencing related emotional difficulties.[30] It might also be presumed that these cadets would be less than completely truthful in admitting to themselves or others how much they may have been affected by the stressfulness of being members of the first group of females ever to enter Annapolis. One officer offered the following comments:

> Can anyone measure the cost of such coping (with stress)? Those who are succeeding as officers might not want to discuss their problem with handling stress, but the problems are there. I wouldn't admit to not being able to handle stress, and some others wouldn't let it show up in a questionnaire or even in an interview.[31]

Women may be so steeled to ongoing scrutiny for signs of deficiency by their male colleagues that they are very cautious about admitting to having experienced stress, lest it be construed as weakness, thereby confirming the stereotype that women are not as able to deal with the difficulties of military service. Being constantly on one's guard in this fashion is in itself stressful.

The way that most career-oriented servicewomen cope with unrealistic performance pressures is to work harder than their male peers. As one female Coast Guard officer stated:

> We have every collateral duty of an engineering officer, and I volunteer for every dirty job that's offered. As a woman, that's important. They say then, 'She's a real engineer'. If I didn't volunteer, they'd say 'she's a woman', but if a man didn't volunteer, or even refused a dirty job they'd say 'He's an officer'.[32]

Some women mention that in a civilian job they wouldn't have the opportunity to really push themselves to discover the limits of their abilities. Other women state that the stress of being pushed to the limits of their abilities is not worth the rewards the military offers them.

6. SEXUAL HARASSMENT

It is impossible to know whether sexual harassment is more prevalent in the military than in the civilian world, although it is apparent that it continues to be a considerable stressor for servicewomen.

In the 1950s the Pentagon established a special civilian panel called the Defense Advisory Committee on Women in the Services (DACOWITS). Today it has 35 civilian members, most of whom are female. In recent years, this body has become more active in investigating alleged abuses and denouncing military practices that are demeaning to women.

In August 1987 DACOWITS conducted one of its periodic investigations, this time on the status of Navy and Marine women in Hawaii and the Far East. The report concluded: Abusive behaviour (from verbal abuse to blatant sexual harassment) continues to exist in both the Navy and Marine Corps.[33]

Each branch of the service has formal regulations that forbid sexual discrimination and harassment and dictate punishment for offenders. As a preventive measure, each branch is supposed to require servicemen to attend workshops aimed at sensitizing men to the issues of sexual harassment and discrimination and familiarizing them with military regulations.

The formal system of prevention, detection and punishment of sexual harassment has produced mixed results. One servicewoman had the following to say:

Sexual harassment continues to be as big a problem today as it was discovered to be in the 1987 DACOWITS study. Women still fail to report sexual harassment incidents for fear of reprisal. Case in point: victims, rather than perpetrators, are still routinely removed from their commands.[34]

It appears that an important factor in whether or not the system is effective in dissuading sexual harassment, has to do with the command climate. If servicewomen happen to find themselves serving under a supportive superior or commander who lets it be known that he or she takes sexual harassment seriously, it is more likely that the command climate will be less tolerant of sexual harassment, and thus less stressful for servicewomen.

7. FRATERNIZATION

Rules governing fraternization exist in all branches of the military service. What this means is that service members of different rank are actively discouraged from socializing or becoming romantically involved. The Army regulation on fraternization reads: 'Relationships between service members of different rank which involve, or give the appearance of partial or preferential treatment...are prejudicial to good order, discipline, and unit morale.'

Fraternization rules can create particular stress for female service members in a number of ways. The overwhelming majority of servicewomen (enlisted members and officers) are single. Since there are roughly nine males to every one female, the pressure for females to be involved in a relationship is quite substantial. For female enlisted service members, the pressure to be involved, particularly with an attentive male of higher rank, may be too compelling.

Second, the stress of being socially isolated which affects female officers is compounded by fraternization rules. One female Coast Guard officer was quoted as saying:

It can get very lonely in a new place with no friends and no family, and you may find that the enlisted crewmen are the only ones around in your spare time. When you're in a situation like this, it's hard to understand why you shouldn't get too friendly with them. Or perhaps you understand, but for your own mental well-being you feel you have to make friends with someone.[35]

Nevertheless, 'making friends' with enlisted servicemen can be viewed negatively by traditionally minded superiors who may deny promotions and favourable evaluations to female officers who do so.

8. HOMOSEXUALITY

Another military regulation which, in practice, concerns servicewomen more than servicemen is the one prohibiting homosexuality. The pertinent Army rule asserts that homosexuality 'seriously impairs the accomplishment of the military mission' and declares it to be 'incompatible with military service'.

In recent years between 1,200 and 1,500 people have been discharged each year for homosexuality. It was published in a recent DACOWITS report that servicewomen are three times more likely than men to be prosecuted or discharged for homosexuality.[36] These figures suggest one of two things: either that homosexual females are overrepresented in the military, or that military prosecutors are more likely to pursue cases where the suspects are female. In either case, women tend to experience more stress as a result of this ruling than do their male counterparts.

For the homosexual woman, there is the fear of being publicly exposed, prosecuted and discharged. For the heterosexual woman, there is the fear of being wrongly accused, prosecuted and discharged. In a climate of this nature, the sexual orientation of all servicewomen tends to be carefully scrutinized, thus making women feel that their privacy is invaded, and that their actions are even further on display.

9. MARRIAGE, PREGNANCY, PARENTHOOD

The stress of combining marriage, family and career is perhaps no more exacting for anyone than for the military woman. It is the nature of military service that demands that it be a service member's first moral allegiance; that military goals come first – before spouse and children. A military lifestyle compromises a traditional marriage and family lifestyle for servicemen and for servicewomen it makes it almost impossible.

In a recent study, women Coast Guard officers were nearly unanimous in saying that their professional lives were rewarding, but their social and personal lives were not as good.[37] The best that female officers can hope for is to marry another officer who shares the same professional and moral commitments, although, as we shall see, this situation is still far from ideal. Compared to US civilian wives, wives in dual-military marriages are somewhat more likely to report lower marital satisfaction.[38]

The military establishment makes an effort to accommodate dual-service couples, but can go only so far as a result of the limitations inherent in carrying out its primary mission. Military 'detailers', whose job it is to coordinate job assignments in accord with current and projected needs of the organization, are required to take marital status into account when fillings 'billets' (jobs). If dual billets are not immediately available, couples may have to wait some months before they can be united. This means that they may spend some time apart, living and working in separate places every couple of years when they change duty stations.

The situation becomes further complicated for married or single service members when they have children. Until 1976 any woman who became pregnant while on active duty was discharged, whether she wanted to be or not. It is now the case that servicewomen who become pregnant may request discharge, and are usually granted permission to leave the armed forces. It is estimated that about one-third of pregnant servicewomen request discharge.[39] If a woman holds a job in a 'critical' skill area for which she has been extensively trained at great expense, her request may be denied. This is not unheard of and, among servicewomen, officers are well aware that they are the most likely candidates for forced retention.

A recent Navy study in San Diego found that 41 per cent of pregnant sailors were single.[40] The Navy and other branches of the armed forces are growing increasingly concerned about how single parents (the overwhelming majority of whom are female) are going to successfully combine the rigours of child-rearing and high performance and long hours in a demanding military job over the long run. Approximately one out of every 11 servicewomen are pregnant at any given time, although it is common knowledge that the military unofficially discourages pregnancy, and suggests that it is a potential roadblock to future advances for servicewomen.[41] Women are given a pregnancy test when they report for basic training. If they are found to be pregnant, they are discharged for a 'preexisting medical condition'. Also, the military no longer allows single parents to enlist if they have custody of their children. Active duty servicewomen who give birth must return to work soon after delivery.

During the Reagan years, legislation was enacted that cut off military funding for elective abortions at US hospitals and clinics. Until very recently abortions at military hospitals were banned as well.[42] This meant that women stationed abroad were required to travel to a civilian hospital at their own expense if they chose to terminate their pregnancies.

Department of Defense officials estimate that there are about 66,000 single parents on active duty who have dependent children and about 47,000 dual-service couples with children.[43] This represents approximately 12.5 per cent of the 2-million-member active duty force. As the number of military service parents has increased, the demand for on-base day care has grown accordingly, although child care has not been made a priority. At the present time there are over 90,000 military dependent children enrolled in 640 child-care centres at 408 different military bases, and there are still waiting lists for admission at most bases. In the Navy alone, there is currently a shortage of at least 25,000 spaces.

Even if a military base has no child-care centre, or no space is available in an existing centre, each service parent is still responsible for ensuring that his or her children are properly cared for during duty hours. Military parents who are found negligent in providing 'proper' child care for their children are subject to prosecution and punishment.

Military parents are also responsible for making sure that their children are cared for in the event that they be sent to war. During the Gulf War, 16,300 single parents and 1,231 dual-service couples with children were deployed to the Middle East.[44] Single parents and dual-service couples are required by military regulations to have contingency plans for child care at all times.

The above illustrations are sufficiently telling to require only brief elaboration or clarification of the stressors inherent in being a married or single servicewoman with children. Primary moral allegiance to the military, long separations from spouses for dual-career couples, limited control over job placement assignments, insufficient and (for lower-ranking servicewomen) costly child-care facilities, personal and financial responsibility for the constant maintenance of long-term child-care contingency plans, separations from families during temporary duty assignments, unofficial dissuasion of pregnancy, and little or no support for termination of pregnancy, are all stressors to which enlisted servicewomen and female officers may be subjected.

Recent studies in the United States and abroad provide strong evidence that certain work conditions, especially having too many demands and too little authority, are associated with the development of stress-related illnesses. Further, these illnesses are more likely to emerge among those who are also experiencing stress at home, especially the stress of rearing children and having a non-supportive husband.[45] A woman who has a demanding, low-status job with little decision-making authority (a good description of the work that most enlisted servicewomen are assigned to) who is married to a man having traditional views of women's and men's roles, may experience lack of authority and excessive demands both at home and at work. Having children and an unsupportive boss may add to the demands she experiences and emphasize her lack of authority in dealing with them.[46]

It has been documented an infinite number of times that women in the United States are still principally responsible for child care and housework. A 1990 *New York Times* poll once again found that, although the situation has improved during the past decade, women still do twice as much housework as men do – 10 hours more a week.[47] There is no reason to assume that these figures do not apply to US servicewomen as well.

10.   A LOOK AT THE FUTURE

When talking with female servicewomen about their situations, one message comes across time and time again: they
don't want to be treated differently from men. They ask only
that they be given the same opportunities as their male
counterparts. Women who take their military careers seriously see themselves as soldiers, sailors, airmen or marines.

One thing has become increasingly evident: women are
not going to go away, in spite of the tremendous stressors
that they face in the military. Declining re-enlistment numbers are expected to level off, enlistment numbers are on the
rise and military women are adamant about being allowed
access to combat jobs. In an informal poll made recently by
the Executive Committee of the Defense Advisory Committee on Women in the Services (DACOWITS), 90 per cent of
the 1,500 to 2,000 women polled said they would like all
military jobs opened to women.[48] Air Force Brigadier General Nora A. Astafan said in an interview that military
leaders will be carefully watching Canada's recent experiment of opening up all armed forces jobs, including seats in
combat aircraft, to women. She added:

> It will be interesting to see how it works. I think it will
> evolve so slowly, and it'll be so effective, that nobody will
> even notice...Cities all over the country have female police
> officers on the streets fighting crime every day. And this
> has become accepted slowly but surely by everyone.[49]

Whether or not women are admitted to combat positions,
they will eventually find themselves acquiring more power in
the military, as the professional servicewomen who entered
during the years of expansion after 1973 gradually ascend in
rank. Lieutenant General Donald Jones, the Pentagon's
uniformed personnel chief, predicted that if the combat
exclusion was fully repealed, women's promotion rates would
remain relatively unchanged, but a greater number would
reach the colonel and general officer grades.[50] Larger numbers of female officers are not likely to have a great impact
on the hierarchical, authoritarian styles of leadership so pre-

valent today, as long as military training continues to be based on reinforcing traditional male norms and values. One positive outcome of having more women in positions of power in the military may be policy changes which are more favourable to women. Probably the biggest change that may be seen as a result of ever-increasing numbers of enlisted servicewomen and female officers will be ongoing attitudinal change towards women on the part of male service members. As has been noted by many psychologists: attitudes may follow, or derive from, behaviours. This has already happened to some degree, as male service members, who increasingly encounter evidence testifying against traditional sex-role stereotypes, continue to exhibit changes in their attitudes towards women. Further, it has been suggested that individuals often behave as a function of their location in organizational structures.[51] If military organizational structures are modified, thus removing the barriers to women's access to power and authority, male service members may begin to regard, and behave towards their female counterparts as less different, more capable, and inevitably more equal.

Notes

1. F. W. Kaslow, *The Military Family* (New York: Guilford Press, 1984).
2. 'U.S. Servicewomen Harassed Overseas', *New York Times*, 21 February 1989.
3. Letter to the editor, *Navy Times*, 11 February 1991.
4. 'The U.S. Marines in 1990', *Naval Institute Proceedings*, May 1991.
5. On 28 April 1993 after this essay was completed, US Defense Secretary Les Aspin ordered the military to allow women to fly aircraft engaged in combat missions.
6. '"Legal" Sexism', Letter to the editor, opinion page, *Navy Times*, 21 January 1991.
7. T. Ensigne, Esq., *Military Life, the Insider's Guide* (New York: Prentice Hall, 1990).
8. 'Women Making Waves in Navy', *Los Angeles Times*, 9 April 1989.
9. Kaslow, *The Military Family*.
10. R. Barnett, 'Women, Work, and Stress: Another Look' in *The Women's Annual Number 5*, 1984–5, ed. Mary Drake McFeely (G. K. Hall Women's Studies Publications).
11. R. Kanter, *Men and Women of the Corporation* (New York: Basic Books, 1977).
12. Ibid.

13. Ibid.
14. L. B. De Fleur and R. L. Warner, 'Air Force Academy Graduates and Non-graduates: Attitudes and Self-Concepts', *Armed Forces and Society*, 13, 4 (1987).
15. *Report from the National Commission on Working Women of Wider Opportunities for Women* (Washington, DC, 1990).
16. W. A. Kahn and F. Crosby, 'Discriminating Between Attitudes and Discriminatory Behaviors, Change and Stasis' in *Women and Work*, An Annual Review, 1 (Beverly Hills, London, New Delhi: Sage, 1985).
17. Ibid.
18. 'A Few Good Women', *Social Issues Resources Series*, 4, article taken from *Savvy* (January 1989).
19. K. P. Durning, 'Attitudes of Enlisted Women and Men Toward the Navy', *Armed Forces and Society*, 9, 1 (Fall 1982).
20. M. Rottman, 'Women Graduates of the U.S. Coast Guard Academy: Views from the Bridge', *Armed Forces and Society*, 11, 2 (1985).
21. Ibid.
22. Kanter, *Men and Women of the Corporation*.
23. 'Feminization of the Military Caldron Still Boils', *Navy Times*, 31 July 1989.
24. A. Craig Copetas, 'Conquering Heroines', *Mirabella*, June 1991.
25. Rottman, 'Women Graduates of the U.S. Coast Guard Academy'.
26. C. Gilligan, *In a Different Voice* (Cambridge: Harvard University Press, 1982).
27. Rottman, 'Women Graduates of the U.S. Coast Guard Academy'.
28. Ensign, Esq., *Military Life*.
29. Rottman, 'Women Graduates of the U.S. Coast Guard Academy'.
30. Ibid.
31. Ibid.
32. Ibid.
33. Ensign, Esq., *Military Life*.
34. '"Legal" Sexism', Letter to the editor, opinion page, *Navy Times*, 21 January 1991.
35. Rottman, 'Women Graduates of the U.S. Coast Guard Academy'.
36. Ensign, Esq., *Military Life*. Since the completion of this essay, military regulations regarding homosexuality have been relaxed considerably.
37. Rottman, 'Women Graduates of the U.S. Coast Guard Academy'.
38. Kaslow, *The Military Family*.
39. Ensign, Esq., *Military Life*.
40. Ibid.
41. Ibid.
42. Ibid.
43. 'Pentagon backs away from Exemption for Mothers of Infants', *Navy Times*, 1 April 1991.
44. Ibid.
45. Barnett, 'Women, Work and Stress'.
46. Ibid.

47. 'The Status of Women and Work in the USA: A *NY Times* Poll', *New York Times,* 20–22 August 1989.

48. 'Jones: Women Say They're Ready to Fill Greater Role', *Army Times,* 27 July 1991.

49. 'Women Making Waves in Navy', *Los Angeles Times,* 9 April 1989.

50. 'Jones: Women Say They're Ready to Fill Greater Role', *Army Times,* 27 July 1991.

51. Kahn and Crosby, 'Discriminating Between Attitudes and Discriminatory Behaviors, Change and Stasis'.

Part II
Uniforms and Chador in the Gulf War

5 The Politics of Constructing the American Woman Soldier

Cynthia H. Enloe

More American women fought in a war zone during the 1990–91 Gulf War than had fought in any American war since the Second World War. The 40,000 white, black, Asian-American and Hispanic American women who were deployed to Saudi Arabia during this nine-month military build-up amounted to four times the number of American military women sent to Vietnam over the entire decade of US involvement in that country. Three-fourths of those women were deployed by the Army. Only 3 per cent of Canada's forces sent to the Gulf were women (though women make up 10.6 per cent of Canada's entire active duty force), while Britain's units were 1.5 per cent women (again lower than the 5 per cent level of its total military). France deployed 13 women in its 10,000-soldier force. Kuwait included 9 women among the 250 Kuwaiti volunteers sent to the US for military training in 1991.[1]

During the August 1990–March 1991 period when the Gulf War was prepared for and waged, there was a torrent of American public attention aimed at 'women in the military'. This sparked a national discussion strikingly akin to the discussions that have occurred in virtually every American war since the eighteenth century. Even when women were used only marginally – e.g. as civilian nurses in military medical services during the 1860–65 Civil War – their participation inspired public anxieties and hopes quite disproportionate to their actual numbers. So too in the Gulf War: American women sent to the Gulf were only 7 per cent of the total US uniformed contingent; and that 7 per cent under-represented women's 11 per cent proportion of the total US uniformed active duty force worldwide.

81

Thus it does not seem to be numbers or proportions that determine whether the American public becomes conscious of the gendered stakes in a given war. Rather, it appears to be women's proximity to this institution that so many Americans deem closer than any other institution to (1) where the *state* and the *nation* converge and (2) where that convergence is suffused with both organized *violence* and selfless *sacrifice*. Violent sacrifice under state discipline in the name of the nation – this seems to get very close to what many Americans, still today at the dawn of the post-Cold War era, understand to be the essential criterion for 'first class citizenship'. If this is so, it makes the doorway into that desired realm narrow indeed.

It also makes that desired realm gendered. For violent sacrifice and state-disciplined service have been imagined in American culture to be masculine domains.[2] What reconciles the unresolved national debate over women's proper place in wartime with the cultural inclination to associate true citizenship with militarized sacrifice? It may be professionalization. If American citizen-soldiering became professionalized – if it can be liberated from its traditional need to be associated with Minute Man amateurism – *and* if professionalization could bestow on American notions of femininity a new coat of protective respectability, then perhaps women could gain access to 'first class citizenship' without jeopardizing the still-gendered political culture. Transforming the feminized meaning of respectability has been a major goal of virtually all women's rights movements in countries as different as Brazil, Russia and the United States. Transformation of gendered militarized respectability seems to be what occurred in American culture between 1972 and 1993.

Participation of women inside the state's military invested the very idea of femininity with extraordinary political saliency. The peculiarities of both how femininity is constructed and how the state's military tries to organize relationships between masculinity and femininity may be distinctively American. But in the dozens of societies for which we have comparable evidence one can see a similar tendency: when the state's military – or an insurgent military aspiring to replace the state – comes to rely on women inside its uniformed ranks, that military provokes wide public concern about the meaning and uses of femininity. This provocation, in turn, makes the content and function of masculinity more problematic.[3]

Post-Cold War era American popular and élite discussions about how to use women and men differentially to serve military purposes have a significance that extends beyond filling out a cross-national comparative analysis.

First, the United States military's gendered manpower formula has had an exceptional influence on other militaries. American military thinking over the past two decades has encompassed not only nuclear strategic doctrine and standardized weapons production, but also ideas on how best to use women in ways that optimize human resources and relegitimize the military during an era of disintegrating power blocs and changing relations between women and men. Given NATO's structure of inequality, these American military ideas have insinuated themselves throughout the 15 member states in the alliance in a way that, say, Dutch or Italian military thinking has not. Having said this, however, it is important to confess that we know all too little about the internal cultural dynamics of institutions such as NATO. This ignorance prevents us as analysts of international political culture to determine how, and if, genuinely new concepts of 'enemy', 'threat', 'security' are trickling though the alliance's bureaucratic layers. Nor can we tell how (I do not believe we have to add an 'if') these possible cultural transformations are reshaping NATO's own gendered culture. We need feminist anthropologists to imagine that 'the field' lies inside NATO's Brussels headquarters.

But NATO is not the only structure that produces the American military's disproportionate influence on ideas about gender. Literally thousands of military officers, especially those tagged by their own superiors for senior promotion and thus policy responsibilities, are trained by American military institutions: the School of the Americas in Panama, Fort Bragg in South Carolina, the Army War College in Carlisle, Pennsylvania, the Navy War College in Newport, Rhode Island, and, of course, the three service academies at

Annapolis, West Point and Colorado Springs. Each of these training institutions has been a conduit for explicit and implicit 'lessons' about how to ensure bonding and morale, how to enforce discipline, how to cultivate leadership, how to optimize human resources in different sorts of warfare. And all of these training preoccupations – bonding, morale, leadership, discipline, human resources management – are profoundly gendered, even if there is not a single woman in the platoon.

Second, the globalization of communications and culture has made the ways in which American military and civilian commentators reassert or redefine presumptions about what is possible within the ideological confines of femininity and masculinity disproportionately influential. Hollywood is not the world's most prolific producer of films: Bombay is. Yet it is Hollywood's films that are the most widely distributed. It is therefore Sylvester Stallone's *Rambo* that is affecting diverse societies' ideas about militarized masculinity, not a Hindi actor's portrayal of a singing warrior prince. Similarly, Goldie Hawn's *Private Benjamin* has spread the image – we do not know how persuasively – of the modern single woman finding fitness and self-assurance in her country's military.[4]

More recently, American-produced satellite television companies have internationalized the image of the militarized American woman. CNN's role in the Gulf War has been much discussed. But left virtually unanalysed has been its impact on popular constructs of the woman soldier. There were in fact several hundred Australian, British, French and Canadian women soldiers deployed in the Gulf on the Allied side of the conflict. But they were rendered almost invisible not only to the rest of the world, but even to their own compatriots because of the dominance of American-generated news. It was the portrayal of American women's military roles – a sanitized portrait, we are now learning – that became the basis for most of the international discussion of 'women-in-the-military' during the war.

This portrait would have been distorted even if that news coverage had been totally immune to governments' censorship and manipulation. But despite CNN's occasionally subversive operation, American news coverage was deeply influenced by the US Defense Department's efforts to get the sort of coverage that would serve its own priorities. Thus, whereas the Pentagon deliberately had restricted news coverage during the 1983 Grenada invasion and the 1989 Panama invasion in part to keep the public at home unalarmed about the already growing utilization of American women as 'near-combat' troops,[5] in the Gulf conflict the same Defense officials decided that much expanded (though less-than-candid) coverage of women sent abroad would bolster popular support for the war. What the American – and British, Portuguese, Egyptian, Indian – publics therefore see of American women soldiers in this or any other war will be largely dependent on what the US officials at the time deem most ideologically palatable and supportive of their own foreign policy objectives. For both of these reasons, the ideological construction of the American woman soldier spills out multiple consequences. It doesn't have to be this way. In the 1990s, NATO could be reorganized so that the US notion of what legitimizes any member military carries less weight throughout the rest of the alliance. Or after European Community integration, NATO might even fade into security insignificance compared to the now hollow, but perhaps soon to be invigorated, Western European Union (WEU) or the increasingly active United Nations peacekeeping forces. At the same time, alternative news and entertainment outlets possibly might challenge the international influence of the US media giants. But until either or both of these transformations occur, the image and reality of American women soldiers calls for special attention, not because they are admirable, but because their images produce such far-reaching cross-national ripples.

The 1990–91 Gulf War may have surprised a lot of Americans who had not paid much attention to the gender transformations taking place inside their military. It even, it seems, surprised many women in uniform, especially reservists. But the developments that made headlines during the war had been in the making since 1972. That was the year that the US Congress ended the male draft, made so unpopular by the long Vietnam War. Fearing that an all-volunteer force would become disproportionately reliant on black men, manpower planners inside the Defense Department and in the powerful Congressional armed services committees, apparently looked to other sources for military recruits. They rediscoved women.[6]

During the period between the end of the Second World War, when most women in uniform were deliberately demobilized, and the end of the Vietnam War in the early 1970s, when those women who were deployed were made virtually invisible,[7] women comprised less than 2 per cent of American uniformed personnel. More importantly, their role in the military had little if any ideological saliency for policy-makers or the general public. Some women who managed to stay in the military, overwhelmingly white women, report that this had its advantages: because their presence was of so little interest, they had more freedom to carve out their own niches, to outmanoeuvre FBI lesbian-baiters.[8] One might imagine, then, that American femininity was demilitarized between 1946 and 1972. It is more accurate, however, to see the militarization of femininity during those years as simply reconstructed upon women's postwar demobilization. During the Second World War there was an awkward tension between, on the one hand, femininity legitimized by direct participation inside explicitly military institutions and, on the other, femininity legitimized by supportive back-stage roles as military wives, girlfriends and daughters on the fringes of those institutions.

During the 1946–72 years femininity was imagined by American government policy-makers and non-government proponents of Cold War culture in a fashion that would harmonize with militarized national security goals. Loyal wives of male engineers working for defence contractors, loyal wives of male officials working in intelligence services – each were upholding forms of feminine behaviour that sustained the Cold War. Likewise, women teaching elementary school children about the dangers of communism, mothers who believed they were doing the right thing to support their sons in accepting their draft call-ups, women who felt proud in doing volunteer work for patriotic organizations such as the Veterans of Foreign Wars – all of them as well were fulfilling this Cold War militarized ideal of American femininity. They all were making the sorts of sacrifices recognized as bestowing 'first class citizenship', but they were proving that they could hold on to their respectability while serving as patriotic mothers and patriotic wives. Thus, as the hot war was replaced by the Cold War in American gendered political culture, there was less ideological confusion over, but not necessarily less militarization of, American femininity.[9]

With the US Government's decision to vastly increase the numbers and proportions of women in the military, to offset the end of the male draft and to forestall a reliance on black male volunteers, a great deal more popular as well as official attention was devoted to the tensions between these two notions of militarized femininity.

The 1972 to 1991 history of how these tensions emerged over American femininity was played out in several arenas simultaneously. It would be easier to make sense of this history, of course, if we could picture each of these different arenas producing ideas that flowed smoothly into and thus reinforced developments in the neighbouring arenas. But we cannot take this for granted. It may very well be that the politics of militarized femininity going on in one arena was relatively unconnected to, or at least at odds with, the gendered trends developing in the others. Perhaps most closely monitored among those arenas where the image of American militarized femininity was being created was that of the media. But, despite all the concentration of American media power in the past 20 years, it remains fragmented enough so that we should consider it in some detail, rather than as a single generator of images of militarized femininity or of the woman soldier.

Within the American media arena, those actors which took part in creating both images were the mass-market print and electronic media (news and fiction), but also the burgeoning specialized media, particularly created by, and directed at, African Americans, Latinos (especially with the build-up of the wars in Nicaragua and El Salvador), feminists of all racial communities, gay men and lesbians, male military veterans and female military veterans (each with their own distinct as well as overlapping magazines and newsletters). Each outlet carried stories about women in 'boot camp' (basic training), women in the service academies, male officers training women recruits, male enlisted men working alongside women as peers, women leaving home for the military, women returning to their communities as veterans, women fighting to stay in the military, women being dismissed from the military. Each story was written or filmed with a particular audience in mind. Two stories about women in boot camp could look very different if one were constructed in order to interest a mostly male veteran readership, while the other was designed to engage a feminist readership.

During the 1972–90 period of growing tensions between the two constructions of American militarized femininity there also were actors in other arenas actively trying to define 'issues' and 'lessons' concerning women's increasing presence in the US military. Chief among those was the Congress. The Congressional Armed Services Committees – particularly the personnel subcommittees in the House and Senate – held repeated hearings on women soldiers in the last two decades. Most were initiated by three women in the House of Representatives, all Democrats and thus able to command considerable committee-level influence: Colorado Democrat Patricia Schroeder, Maryland Democrat Beverly Byron (defeated in her 1992 re-election bid) and California Democrat Barbara Boxer (now one of California's two women senators). It matters that, while the Defense Department did not initiate its 1970s post-draft energetic recruitment of women due to Congressional women's pressure, by the time those new generations of women recruits were being noticed by the popular media in the late 1980s, there were enough women in Congress (the great majority in the House of Representatives, only two then in the Senate) with enough seniority to have an impact on the legislative construction of women soldiers.

On the other hand, these Congressional hearings did not attract coverage from the most influential television networks, popular news weeklies, wire services or big city newspapers. When the House Military Personnel and Compensation Subcommittee of the Committee on Armed

Services held its post-Panama hearings in March, 1990, on women in the military, it was far, far from being a media event on the scale of the Clarence Thomas–Anita Hill hearings. While they were monitored by some women's advocacy groups and by the Defense Department, they barely caused a stir in the news outlets that affect the political consciousnesses of ordinary Americans.[10]

Sometimes called to testify before these Congressional committees have been representatives of high-school career counsellors' organizations, black civil rights groups, peace organizations, civil liberties lawyers and gay rights groups. During the past two decades, when the proportions of women recruited into the military grew from a mere 2 per cent to a substantial – and very visible – 11 per cent, each of these organized interest sectors paid only sporadic, but occasionally concentrated, attention to issues that involved women in the military. In doing so, their leaders sometimes shaped the lens through which people identifying with a particular profession or movement thought about women as soldiers. Just as often, however, the attention paid remained relatively confined to specialists within each of these sectors. For instance, although a prominent black civil rights research centre organized a conference in the mid-1980s to bring together civil rights leaders and Defense Department officials to discuss the particular problems facing blacks in the military, relatively little attention was directed to the rapidly growing numbers of black women enlistees, and the conference did not set off in its wake discussions among ordinary members of the black community about the 'black woman soldier.[11]

Most American feminist groups have paid scant attention to the issue of women in the military. Indeed, it has been the emergence of peace activism within the 1970s–1980s women's movement that has made the issue of women in the military either seem to be trivial or ideologically awkward. Where feminists have focused on women soldiers, they have been inclined to reconcile conflicting values by portraying the woman soldier as a poor woman who volunteers for military service not out of a desire to earn the status of American patriot or out of any commitment to the Reagan or Bush administration's global interventionism, but out of the apolitical desire to obtain an income, training and health benefits fast disappearing elsewhere in an era of high defense spending, public service cuts and economic recession. While this portrait may have been correct, most feminist groups did not feel that the image of woman soldier was significant enough to devote their very scarce resources to checking that image against reality. This presumption and inattention, while understandable, left many feminists active in anti-nuclear, Central American and Middle Eastern peace work (the principal areas of American feminist peace activism during the 1970s–1980s) unprepared for the politics of gendered image-making during the Gulf War.

It was the classically liberal women's advocacy organizations with national agendas and offices in Washington, for instance the National Organization of Women, the Women's Research and Education Institute and particularly the now defunct Women's Equity Action League, that did investigate the realities of the lives of women soldiers. Each of these organizations collected data on military women and addressed issues concerning fairness in their newsletters. They deliberately intervened in court, legislative and executive deliberations that shaped ideas about militarized femininity, deliberately trying to shape male state officials' perceptions of femininity. They used the concept of first class citizenship in ways reminiscent of the woman suffragists two generations earlier.

Questions about peace or militarism were less likely to be raised. These groups seemed to feel most comfortable when they could treat equality inside the military institution and the Government's use of the military overseas as questions belonging in separate compartments. On the other hand, more than some other feminist groups, these Washington-based feminists were more curious about and sensitive to the race and class diversity of women beginning to enlist in the newly welcoming military. They were less likely to portray all women volunteers as victims of the 'poverty draft'. And they were more attentive to relationships between men and women inside the military, taking up issues of sexual harassment and masculinized divisions of labour more systematically than were feminists working in the peace movement.

Consequently, it would be these groups who would be best prepared after the Gulf War to respond to what became the infamous 'Tailhook scandal' involving grand-scale sexual harassment. It was also to the women in these Washington-based liberal women's organizations (and to a handful of feminist academics known to these groups) that mainstream television and press reporters turned when constructing images of the woman soldier in August 1990.[12]

The Department of Defense is itself a complex mesh of interlocking but not-always harmonious ideological actors. In both defining and supporting the post-1972 woman soldier, DACOWITS (the Defense Advisory Committee On Women In The Armed Services) has been the pre-eminent 'DOD' actor. Created during the Korean War, when the Government was using few women but wanted to assure the public that those it needed were conforming to American Cold-War conventions of feminine respectability, DACOWITS is made up of prominent civilian women (and now military officers as well) and reports directly to the Secretary of Defense. Although filled during the 1980s with Republican women appointees, women who generally rejected any affiliation with 'feminism', DACOWITS gradually became activist in its own term. Its members adopted a mandate to search out and publicly report sexist barriers to women's advancement in the three branches of the military. It did so in the name of optimizing national security and military 'readiness'. The Cold War against the Soviet Union and the communist threat in general could not, DACOWITS argued, be effectively waged if women soldiers' full talents were not used and rewarded. 'Readiness' soon became the criterion wielded by all Washington insiders who tried to influence military personnel policies during the Reagan years.

While DACOWITS had few connections with civil rights, peace or feminist groups and thus had minimal impact on their perceptions of the woman soldier, it did have a political status that got them a hearing among Defense Department senior officials, Congressional armed service committee members, Washington-based liberal women's organizations and, occasionally, the national press. DACOWITS obtained for women soldiers' equity concerns a certain political legitimacy. A woman soldier in DACOWITS' eyes was not a victim of the 'poverty draft'. She was, instead, a competent female citizen whose public contributions to national defence and whose respectability as a woman were being jeopardized by male soldiers' sexual harassment, male superiors' complacency, and antiquated bureaucratic rules that were out of step with changes in technology and battlefield doctrine. In the process, DACOWITS may have been an architect of the image of the American woman soldier that was ready to be disseminated at the outset of the Gulf War: the woman soldier as a still-feminine, professionalized 'citizen-patriot'.[13]

There were a multitude of ideological players with which DACOWITS engaged inside the corridors of the Pentagon. By the 1970s, the department's Equal Opportunity office was fully institutionalized, if not always equipped with bureaucratic clout. The civilian presidentially appointed Under Secretary for Manpower and Logistics, by contrast, had ready access to the Secretary and to Congressional committees. Although Republicans within an administration that was singularly uninterested in women's issues, the men filling this position generally supported the proposition that the military needed women to enlist – and re-enlist.

Unlike its Canadian and the British counterparts, the US military continues to be organized into bureacratically separate, often rival, services. Thus the ideological discourses and actual policies derived from notions about militarized femininity are sometimes quite different in the Navy, Air Force, Army and Marines. For instance, many military insiders were not surprised when it was the Navy that was home to the men who threw the misogynist Tailhook party in Las Vegas in September 1991. Not only the Navy's carrier pilots ('tailhookers'), with their celebrated sense of masculine bravado, but the entire Navy had the reputation of being especially protective of its exclusivist male culture.[14] One witness before the House Armed Services Committee noted during hearings called to investigate the Tailhook scandal that perhaps more indicative of the Navy's institutional resistence to giving up their historically masculinized culture was what went on in Las Vegas *before* the much-publicized party. At what the Tailhook convention organizers billed as a professional seminar, 'an admiral crawled under a table to avoid answering a female officer's question about opportunities for women pilots'. As the witness, Edwin Dorn of the Brookings Institution, a respected monitor of the American military's treatment of blacks, went on to explain to the Congressional representatives, the admiral 'thought the gesture was funny; and it probably was to the men in the audience who were sporting "not in my unit" buttons. An officer who responded so dismissively to a question about a racial issue probably would have been disciplined'.[15]

The deeply institutionalized defensiveness that permeated the Navy was uncovered when an independent investigation was ordered of the Navy's own mismanaged initial investigation of the infamous Tailhook convention. The Defense Department's Office of Inspector General found that the Navy's own effort to find out what happened in Las Vegas, and why, was seriously flawed due to senior investigatory officers' desire to protect not just particular colleagues but their own institution from outside criticism. In a particularly damning episode, described in detail by the the review's author, the Defense Department's Deputy Inspector General, the commander of the Naval Investigative Service(NIS), an admiral, held what witnesses described as a 'screaming match' in a Pentagon's corridor with a senior civilian woman official, an Assistant Secretary of the Navy. The civilian official had protested when the admiral, a key figure in controlling the direction of the initial investigation of the Tailhook affair, opined that 'a lot of female Navy pilots are go-go dancers, topless dancers or hookers'.[16] At another time during the Navy's own attempt to look into the affair, the same admiral was told by one of his own agents that a women officer assaulted during the convention had recalled saying to her attackers, 'What the fuck do you think you're doing?' To which the admiral responded ('and', the woman NIS agent told a later investigator, 'I'll remember this quote forever') 'Any woman that would use the F word on a regular basis would welcome this type of activity'.[17]

Air Force policy-makers, with their service's relatively high proportion of support roles (e.g. many mechanics and flight controllers for a single fighter pilot), found that they could recruit large numbers of women without jeopardizing the masculinized construction of its combat élite. By contrast, American Marines officers feared that even a small proportion of women in its combat-heavy service would threaten its deeply masculinized image. The Army, of course, includes under its institutional roof the combat units of infantry and armoured divsions. But it also stands out because of its 'manpower' neediness. Thus the US Army, like armies in most countries, tend to be the most ethnically and economically diverse, though that diversity may be carefully arranged hierarchically. It has to recruit such large numbers of people that it cannot be as selective as the other services, and its male recruits in particular tend to be quite young and immature.[18]

The male officers in the field commanding troops in the 1970s and 1980s often were far more ambivalent than their civilian Defense Department superiors about the wisdom or need of women deployed in traditionally masculinized jobs. Many – not all – of these officers were more concerned about the morale of their men, men who had been recruited partly with the promise that joining the military would confirm their manliness. Some of these male officers had access to the press, particularly the media aimed at veterans, and to Congressional committees. They too wielded the potent national security concept of 'readiness', but they used it to argue that women had no place at the front and that those women who wanted to be there were raising questions about their own femininity and patriotism.[19]

And finally there were the women soldiers themselves. Though 'soldiers' is a somewhat misleading term here. For many women, like many men, who joined the uniformed forces deliberately sought out jobs as administrators, computer technicians, nurses and nutritionists, jobs that were militarized but which did not jar the masculinization of American soldiering or their own internalized feminine identities. A 1992 survey of 868 Army women, one of the largest of its kind and solicited by the presidentially appointed Commission on the Assignment of Women in the Military, revealed that while 60 per cent of women officers and 54 per cent of women enlisted personnel wanted the ban on women in combat, they were not necessarily imagining themselves as combat volunteers. They themselves, like many men, wanted training, education, separation from families, a steady income, not the opportunity to wield instruments of direct violence. Only 15 per cent of the Army women surveyed in the aftermath of the Gulf War expressed a desire to serve in combat roles. What they wanted most, they said, were institutional reforms that would remove the barriers currently barring women from promotions. The combat ban, they reported, was the spikiest barrier.[20]

Women in uniform themselves did not have a monolithic image of their own femininity or of the military's impact on it. Women career officers, for instance, tended to be those most outspoken about existing bans on women in 'combat'. It was they who saw themselves staying in the service for 20 years and so tagged combat-exclusion as a principal barrier to their promotions. Enlisted women often were more frustrated by day-to-day harassment, and by the military's inadequate medical services for women. They were the women soldiers with perhaps the biggest stake in insuring that veterans' health and educational benefits were designed to fit women veterans' needs and were sustained by a budget-conscious Congress.

One gets the impression that it was the women careerists, officers, who were more likely to have the confidence and the contacts to speak out when they felt they were being harassed or being denied a hearing by their immediate superiors. It has been the women officers that have been most apt to be in contact with the liberal women advocates in Washington, who have been more likely to be interviewed by Congressional subcommittees and television talk show hosts, thus privileging their concerns and their experiences in this complex cultural political process that was creating the image of the American woman soldier. And because only 19 per cent of all women officers in the early 1990s are black women,[21] it has been white women careerists' ideas that have tended to receive the most visibility.

These diverse, segmented, yet occasionally overlapping or dependent American image-making arenas are worth spelling out. Looking at each of them separately reminds us that the ideology of militarized femininity has not been constructed through some simple or obvious process in either the Cold War or the post-Cold War era. It also alerts us to ask hard questions about how the image of the woman soldier is constructed and reconstructed in other countries as well.

- Do Japanese or Norwegian journalists from the mainstream national media call on field officers to voice their opinions on their women soldiers?
- Is there the equivalent of the House of Representatives Armed Services Subcommittee on Personnel in France or Turkey?
- Do women's groups with equal opportunity agendas have comparable access to their countries' defence ministries' manpower bureacrats in Britain or Italy?
- Have gay liberation activists turned their attention to homophobia inside the military in either Israel or India?
- Do racial minority rights organizations monitor discrimination inside the military with the help of state-established agencies in Canada or Germany?
- Do Australian or Dutch base commanders agree with most American base commanders' decision to carry pornographic magazines on their base newstands?[22]

For all the outpouring of recent feminist scholarship on the Second World War, we still today scarcely have a complete picture of the interactive processes that redefined and/or entrenched American femininity and masculinity to suit wartime needs in the 1940s. But what we have learned from this burgeoning work is that those earlier ideological processes involved very particular actors with their own anxieties, resources and limitations. It is with this awareness that we need to turn our attention to the construction of images of American – or any other country's – women soldiers in the Gulf War.

The military operations that preceded the Gulf War were the occasions for several of these ideological arenas of the 1980s to touch one another in ways that highlighted the contradictions between the two forms of militarized American femininity. The 1983 invasion of Grenada and the 1989 invasion of Panama became – quite self-consciously – gendered precursors to Operation Desert Storm.

Whereas DACOWITS, Defense Department civilian officials, military male and female officers, Congressional committees, specialized academic researchers and Washington-based liberal women's advocacy groups were the principal actors shaping the image of the woman soldier between 1972 and 1983, the Grenada invasion opened up the regendered military to wider popular view. This was on the minds of Defense Department public relations officials when they did their best to limit the mainstream media's coverage of women's roles in the invasion. In fact, those roles were wider – closer to the masculinized inner sanctum of 'combat' – than many members of the American public realized, due to the skilful internal lobbying of a handful of women officers. By 1983 these women had both become committed to making senior grades and had learned that the obstacles put in the way of their careerist aspirations could only be surmounted by leap-frogging over their immediate superiors.

From Fort Bragg, the main launching point for the Grenada invasion, several women officers, who saw that they were going to be separated from their assigned units and thus deprived of the chance to take part in the Caribbean operation, called officals in Washington insisting that such a policy was not only unfair to women but threatened to undermine the much-valued *esprit de corps* within the divided units. Eventually, 170 American women soldiers took part in the invasion – as military police, as helicopter pilots, as interrogators, as signal corps specialists, as truck drivers and as members of bomb teams.[23]

The Panama invasion six years later was, for many of these same women careerists and their Washington supporters, a logical next step in forcing a regendering of battle manoeuvres. But this time, press and television media refused to be kept so safely at a distance. The result was much wider coverage and more popular debate over women's proper roles in the military.

The discussion, however, was affected by the overall cultural politics of the Panama invasion. Women were indeed revealed now to be inching closer than ever to masculinized front-line roles, but it was in a war that had broad American public support and was portrayed as short and 'clean'. The spectre of 'Vietnam', a war that tainted the image of the entire military, a war that was seen by many Americans as besmerching, even corrupting any American soldier who took part in it, was being rolled back in Panama. Neither soldiers taking drugs nor soldiers frequenting prostitutes made the headlines during the Panama invasion. There were no stories told of rape. Consequently, it seemed less threatening to respectable femininity for 800 American women soldiers to be involved in this latest war. Military operations in 1989 would be morally just and professionally conducted. Women soldiers' own femininity in the eyes of many Americans could be sustained even close to the front lines if they conducted themselves professionally and if their behaviour leant new respectability to America in the world.

The most widely reported incident treading – and defining – this fine line during the Panama invasion was Captain Linda Bray's leading a small team of male soldiers to take a hostiley held Panamanian military dog kennel. Was she in 'combat'? The question was politically salient enough to have to be responded to by the President's own press officer. The Defense Department claimed that Captain Bray's operation was not combat, that the military was upholding the long-standing ban on women in combat. The press and the general public were less sure. But there was no popular delegitimation of the war following the Bray story. Instead, there was new activism on the part of women in Congress to dismantle the combat ban altogether since the Panama invasion showed how artificial it was and how accepting the American public was of women serving in front-line roles if they did so voluntarily and with professional competence. But inside the military, in field units where so much of the daily construction of women soldiers occurs, Linda Bray experienced new pressures. She and her unit were subjected to investigations (which found no misdeeds); she was mistrusted by her troops who resented all the media attention she had received; she tried to match the men she served with physically and ultimately broke her hip. In April 1991, with no media notice, Linda Bray left the military.[24]

The stage was now set for American image-making during the 1990–91 Persian Gulf War.

Women made up 12 per cent of the total military active duty force. Black, Latino, Asian-American and Native American women together made up 38 per cent of all women in the four branches. But it was the Army that stood out: among the Army's enlisted women, black women had signed up and re-enlisted in such extraordinary numbers in the 1980s that on the eve of the Gulf War they had become 47 per cent of those ranks of women – that is, four times their proportion of all women in American society.[25]

When the Bush administration deployed thousands of troops to Saudi Arabia following the Iraqi invasion of Kuwait, there were none of the attempts witnessed in 1983 to cull women out of units that might serve in near-combat roles. That gender battle had been won.

The Pentagon seemed more confident that the military's public legitimacy would not be undermined if it allowed the mainstream mass media to cover women soldiers. It was emboldened by public opinion polls that showed a majority in favour of widening women's military roles. The result was a flood of stories about American women in the Gulf. The great majority of them were positive. Now we know, however, that stories of rape and assault by American male soldiers on their female comrades were silenced. But during the war, when the massive viewing audience assured maximum media influence, women soldiers were portrayed as 'doing a job' and in so doing enhancing the country's military competence. They were professionals. Even women reservists and enlisted women, many of whom were not professionals in the sense of intending a military career, were portrayed as 'professionals'.

This is an accolade that carries great positive value in an American society in which formal education and publically conferred licensing have come to be seen as guarantors of social respect and economic success. To be a 'pro' means one is taken seriously. In the post-draft American militarized culture, being a professional was no longer at odds with being a citizen-patriot. Professionalism also provided a protective shield, a new form of guaranteed respectability. A professionalized woman soldier, it appeared, was neither morally loose or suspiciously manly. The media stories dealt with the latter anxiety, so common in the Second World War, by emphasizing husbands, children and boyfriends left behind. When Major Rhonda Cornum, a year after the war, finally admitted that she had been sexually assaulted by one of her Iraqi captors, she went to great lengths to explain to journalists that she had downplayed this admittedly unpleasant incident because, as a professional soldier, a flight surgeon and an officer, she counted other challenges she faced as a prisoner of war, for instance, protecting military information and bolstering the morale of her male subordinate, more important than worrying about her sexual well-being.[26]

Assisting in this image-making was the seeming sexual order of the Gulf War. Unlike the US–Vietnam War, which was filled with stories of prostitutes, rape and drugs, this war was under strict sexual control. But it was not imposed by the US government. It was a sexual order insisted upon by the Saudi regime of King Fahd. Fearing that its own internal fundamentalist opposition would exploit any rumours of sexual promiscuity to challenge the regime's political legitimacy, the Saudi Government required that the US government prohibit both alcohol and prostitution in its Saudi operations. This was a highly unusual, perhaps unique, agreement for the US military to enter into. No other American ally had managed to impose such a condition. It seemed to further guarantee that American women could serve as soldiers in this war without losing their feminine respectability. Only a year after the troops – and the camera crews – had gone home, would American women soldiers begin to tell stories which made it clear that the ban on alcohol and brothels did not provide a watertight guarantee that American women in the field would not suffer indignities at the hands of their comrades.[27]

The most controversial aspect of mobilizing 40,000 women in a force of 500,000 Americans to fight in Saudi Arabia was motherhood. If there was one media story theme that momentarily shook the American military's gendered legitimacy it was the story of the mother-as-soldier leaving behind an infant child in the care of a 'mere' father or perhaps a grandmother.

The public had not realized that the Defense Department over recent years had begun to plan for a time when the active duty forces would be subjected to personnel cuts by an increasingly budget-conscious Congress. The Department's personnel planners had started to integrate the Reserves into their regular battle-planning. The Reserves are made up of men and women, many of them veterans of active duty forces, who hold civilian jobs during the week and commit themselves to military duty several weekends each month. The Reserves hold several attractions, not the least among them extra pay. In an era when many young families could not meet mortgage and car payments without the contribution of two salaries per nuclear household, pay from military Reserve duty looked as though it provided just that much-more-than-welcome financial cushion – with virtually no risk. It actually was a necessary source of income to make middle-class ends meet. In addition, women had discovered that they could satisfy their desire to take part in unusual physical activities and to perhaps acquire new skills without having to choose between military participation and having a family. With the Pentagon's blessing – military couples reduce rival loyalties – growing numbers of wives and husbands had enlisted together in the Reserves in the past decade. By the eve of the Gulf War, women had risen to 13 per cent of all military reserve soldiers.

So when the Pentagon began calling up whole reserve units from around the country, many young women found themselves having to leave behind very small children. The media treated this with surprise and dismay.

But the two stories that many observers were anticipating would shatter the apparent acceptance of women in such proximity to battle – women being taken prisoner and 'women coming home in body bags' – did not have the negative effects that were expected. And it wasn't for lack of coverage. Two American women became prisoner of war and both survived, even if they engaged in self-censorship when initially describing their ordeals. Eleven women died in the war, five in combat. It would appear that these events had an effect quite contrary to that foreseen by many nervous policy-makers. For these women's experiences made clearer than ever that being confined to 'non-combat' jobs was not assured protection from capture and even death, given the weaponry of contemporary warfare. Feminist observers had been pointing out the mythical quality of the 'front' and 'rear' distinction for a decade, but now the general public could see it for itself. Instead, the American military women who died had the chance to prove that women, like men, could 'die for their country'. Violence participated in under state discipline for the sake of sacrifice for the nation – this remained the norm for American 'first-class citizenship'. That did not seem to change.

The American image that came out of the Gulf War was of the professionalized woman militarized patriot. This was an image that liberal women's advocates in the Congress, in DACOWITS, in the officer corps and in Washington lobbying organizations had been constructing and promoting for the past two decades. The image that fitted feminist peace activists' perception of the US state and its role in the world – the woman joining up to escape poverty – did not gain much credence in the popular culture as a result of this war. This must give pause to those feminists – feminists who supply the intellectual context and energy for campaigns and institutions all over the country – who believe militarism is integral to American patriarchy.

In the aftermath of the withdrawal of most American forces from the Gulf, the politics of image-making has reverted to its previous arenas. Again it is Congress, DACOWITS, women officers, women's liberal organizations and now, increasingly, gay and lesbian legal rights advocates who are the principal players. Thus, at the initiative of women in the House of Representatives but with the support of several key liberal male Senators, Congress passed, in August 1991, an amendment to the Defense appropriations bill that would end the formal ban on women flying combat airplanes. The actual assignment of women to fighters and bombers, however, was deliberately left by the politically savvy architects of the amendment to the civilian chiefs of the Air Force and Navy. They instructed President George Bush to appoint a commission to study the whole question of women in combat and transmit their conclusions to both the President and the Pentagon.[28] None of the anti-militarism feminist groups took part in this postwar Congressional legislative process. The revelations of Rhonda Cornum's rape while a prisoner of war might have made the bill's designers soon wish that they had left the White House and the armed services with less discretion. Focusing on her experience rather than on those of American non-combat women assaulted by their fellow soldiers permitted the majority of the presidential commission and conservative senior officers once again to dig in their heels.

The history of the presidential commission underscores the ways in which women in combat is a concept shaped and reshaped by the gendered politics of an entire political system. The congressionally legislated, presidentially appointed Commission on the Assignment of Women in the Military consisted of 15 members. George Bush and his aides chose its appointees in early 1992 at a time when the lessons of the Gulf War seemed less salient than the centre-right rivalries inside the President's own political party. From the start, those liberal feminists monitoring the Commission believed that several appointees were deliberately intended to assuage the ideological anxieties of the Republican party's right wing, a wing being courted in the February primaries by conservative candidate Patrick Buchanan. For instance, Bush selected nine men and only six women for the Commission, and among the women were Elaine Donnelly, a member of Phyllis Schlafly's Eagle Forum, and Kate O'Brien, a senior vice president of the conservative Heritage Foundation. According to one of the Women's Research and Education Institute representative, 'Some of these people are really members of the ultra-right would would prefer to have women go home and bake cookies...By appointing a number of these individuals, the President has preordained a decision that would preclude women from serving in combat'.[29]

After six months of study costing $4million, the Commission announced its recommendations on election day, 3 November 1992, when most media attention was turned elsewhere. Only Defense officials and Pentagon-watchers, among them the most stalwart civilian and uniformed advocates of women soldiers' rights, attended the press conference.[30] For many in the audience, the Commission's most surprising recommendation was that women continue to be prohibited from flying combat aircraft. This was clear rejection of the congressional women reformers' principal recommendation: they had selected it as an opening wedge leading to an eventual lifting of the ban on women in all combat jobs. On this first recommendation, the Commission's members had split 8 to 7. The vote was along ideological, not gender lines. Donnelly and O'Brien, the two conservative women voted against women serving as combat pilots on the grounds that women were not meant to be killers. Two of the men who voted for the lifting of this ban were the Commission's head, Robert T. Herres, a retired Air Force general and former vice chairman of the Joint Chiefs of Staff, and Marine Corps Brigadier General Thomas V. Draude who spoke with emotion of his support of his own daughter who was training to be a Navy pilot. 'I'm asked, would you let your daughter fly in combat with the possibility of her becoming a P.O.W.?...And my answer is yes, because I believe we should send the best'.[31]

As expected, the Commission's majority voted to continue the exclusion of women from ground combat jobs, such as those in the infantry and armoured divisions. On the question of women's assignment to naval combat ships, the majority initially sided with exclusion. Then the Commission head, General Herres, appealed to the members to give something to the reformers. If the Commission didn't show a willingness to grant some new service opportunities to women, he argued, 'A great number of people will not believe we credibly considered the issues.' Soon afterwards, the members voted 8 to 6 to amend their recommendation to allow women to serve on combat ships except for amphibious vessels and submarines.[32]

One of the observers in the audience was Lieutenant Paula Coughlin. She was the admiral's aide who was the first military woman to formally charge male Navy combat pilots with sexual harassment in the wake of the 1991 Las Vegas Tailhook Association convention. Upon hearing the Commis-

sion's recommendations, she told a reporter, 'I think the com-
position of the commission was predetermined and selected
for just this outcome'.[33]

The Commission was only a recommending body. Its recommendations were to be sent to the President and to the
Secretary of Defense. Both were about to be transformed as a
result of the Clinton victory. The Clinton White House, on
the one hand, would be under no political obligation to follow
the advice of conservatives and would be actively pressured
to end all combat exclusion by many of the liberal women's
rights groups that backed his campaign; on the other hand,
the new President already was risking high-ranking military
officers' anger with his announced intention to end the ban
on homosexuals in the military. In Congress, a leading pro-
ponent of women soldiers' expanded career opportunites,
Barbara Boxer, now was a senator and backed by many of the
liberal feminist groups that supported an end to the combat
ban, but she had little seniority in the upper House. Patricia
Schroeder remained in the House of Representatives with
the sort of seniority that translated into an armed service
subcommittee chair's position; she was now joined by 39
other women representatives, most of whom defined themselves as feminists. The 'lessons' of the Gulf War remained
fodder for inter-branch, inter-party and inter-ideological
political manoeuvres.

In another arena, however, the feminist Congresswomen's
inability to compel the Defense Department to revise its
gendered war-making formula failed much more quickly.
Then-Representative Barbara Boxer introduced legislation to
force the Pentagon to end its practice of calling up for active
duty women and men with very young infants. However, the
military won the legislative day. Its counter-argument that in
a new era of reduced military manpower it would need
optimum flexibility with all of its personnel persuaded
Boxer's colleagues to drop her amendment from the post-
Gulf legislative agenda. A third arena, gay and lesbian legal
rights groups, stepped up their pressure to force the Defense
Department to end its ban on homosexuals. They too used
the Gulf War to make their point. These spokespeople
claimed that, with educated military manpower in short

supply, the military did in the 1990s what it did at the height of the Second World War: it used all competent soldiers, conveniently turning a blind eye towards suspected gays and lesbians in the ranks. Thus these legal activists came away from the Gulf War hoping that court actions that were slowly whittling away at the rationale for the ban, plus the support of a President newly elected with a decisive gay vote, would together move the Government to end the ban altogether. Their goal: to allow homosexual Americans access to the sort of military service that remains in the United States the *sine qua non* for 'first-class citizenship'.[34]

When the popular media turned its attention to the faltering American domestic economy and when most of the country's advocacy and service feminist organizations were feeling both ideologically stymied by the issue of women soldiers and stretched thin trying to meet their primary commitments – commitments that seemed distant from military issues. It seemed likely, in the early 1990s, that the image-making politics surrounding women in the American military would continue to be in the hands of those who felt comfortable with professionalized militarized femininity. The ideal American woman soldier of the 1990s still wears lipstick in the Pentagon advertisements. Her eyebrows remain neatly plucked. But she isn't smiling. She doesn't put up with harassment. But she also doesn't have much patience with talk of post-Cold War militarism. Under her helicopter pilot's high-tech helmet, she is a serious citizen doing her job; she's a pro.

Notes

1.   C. Becraft, 'Women in the US Armed Services: The War in the Persian Gulf', Women's Research and Education Institute, 1700 18th Street, NW, Suite 400, Washington, DC 20009, March 1991, p. 1. See also 'Women in the Military: What Role Should Women Play in the Shrinking Military?', *CQ Quarterly*, Congressional Quarterly, 2, 36, 25 September 1992, p. 842.

2.   Two recent explorations into the specifically American history of militarized thinking about citizenship are: L. K. Kerber, 'May All Our Citizens Be Soldiers and All Our Soldiers Citizens: The Ambiguities of Female Citizenship in the New Nation', in J. E.

Bethke and S. Tobias (eds) *Women, Militarism and War* (Savage: Rowman and Littlefield, 1990); also M. E. Kann, *On the Man Question: Gender and Civic Virtue in America* (Philadelphia: Temple University Press, 1991).

3. One of the best cross-national collections is: Eva Isaksson (ed.) *Women and the Military System* (London and New York: Harvester Wheatsheaf, 1988.) Other cross-national comparisons can be found in: S. Macdonald, P. Holden and S. Ardener (eds) *Images of Women in Peace and War* (London: Macmillan and Madison: University of Wisconsin Press, 1987); Elshtain and Tobias (eds) *Women, Militarism and War*; N. Loring Goldman (ed.) *Female Soldiers – Combatants or Noncombatants?* (Westport: Greenwood Press, 1982). A useful bibliography of journal articles published in English between 1980–1990 on women and militaries appears in *Journal of Women's History*, 3, 1, 1991, pp. 141–58.

4. A cultural analysis of the 'Private Benjamin' image came out of an international conference of European, Israeli and North American women, the results of which are contained in W. Chapkis (ed.) *Loaded Questions: Women and the Military* (Amsterdam and Washington: Transnational Institute, 1981).

5. A. Fuentes, 'Equality, Yes – Militarism, No', *The Nation*, 28 October 1991, p. 516.

6. This is an hypothesis and has not yet been confirmed by detailed research. I have spelled it out in more detail in *Does Khaki Become You? The Militarization of Women's Lives* (London and New York: Pandora/Harper-Collins, 1988).

7. For descriptions and oral histories of American women who served in the US military in Vietnam, see K. Marshall, *In the Combat Zone* (New York: Penguin, 1987); K. Walker, *A Piece of My Heart* (New York: Ballantine, 1985); L. Van Devanter, *Home Before Morning* (New York: Beaufort, 1983).

8. The Second World War and immediate postwar ups and downs of US military attention to, and harassment of, lesbians and gay men is charted in A. Berube's *Coming Out Under Fire* (New York: Plume/Penguin, 1991).

9. A provocative account of the demands on military wives and especially daughters to conform to those standards of femininity that best served American needs during the 1960s and 1970s has recently been published by a journalist who herself grew up as a military daughter: M. Wertsch, *Military Brats: The Legacy of Childhood Inside the Fortress* (New York: Crown, 1991).

10. 'Women in the Military', hearing before the Military Personnel and Compensation Subcommittee of the Committee on Armed Services of the House of Representatives, 20 March 1990, Washington, DC, US Government Printing Office.

11. The book coming out of this conference is E. Dorn (ed.) *Who Defends America? Race, Sex and Class in the Armed Forces* (Washington, DC, Joint Committee for Political and Economic Studies 1989).

12. Although the Women's Equity Action League died for lack of funding in the late 1980s, its valuable newsletter is available at the Schlesinger Library of Women's History, Radcliffe College, Cambridge, Massachusetts. The guiding spirit of 'WEAL's' Women in the Military Project and one of Washington's most skilled insider lobbyists, C. Becraft, has recently revived this project within the Women's Research and Equity Institute, 1700 18th Street NW, Washington, DC 20009.

13. The first serious feminist analysis of DACOWITS is M. Fainsod Katzenstein's 'Feminism Within American Institutions: Unobtrusive Mobilization in the 1980s', *Signs*, 16, 1, pp. 27–24. Her full-length book comparing feminists inside the US Defense Department and feminists inside the American Catholic Church is forthcoming. M. Katzenstein is a Professor of Government at Cornell University, Ithaca, New York.

14. For detailed accounts of the so-called Tailhook affair, see E. Schmitt, 'Dozens of Women Sexually Assaulted at Pilots Meeting, Navy Finds', *New York Times*, 1 May 1992; E. Schmitt, 'Wall of Silence Impedes Inquiry Into a Rowdy Navy Convention', *New York Times*, 14 June 1992; J. Lancaster, 'Navy Officer Tells of Pilots' Attack on Her in Vegas', *International Herald Tribune*, 25 June 1992; E. Schmitt, 'Now at Navy's Bridge, Engaging Sexism', 4 July 1992; E. Goodman, 'The "Friendly Fire" of Sexual Assault', *Boston Globe*, 5 July 1992; E. Schmitt, 'Officials Say Navy Tried to Soften Report', *New York Times*, 8 July 1992; E. Schmitt, 'Harassment Questions Kill 2 Admirals' Promotions', *New York Times*, 18 July 1992; 'Pentagon Given Film of Harassment, Report Says', *New York Times*, 30 July 1992; J. Drinkard, 'Navy Failed to Act Against Harassment, Admiral Says', *Boston Globe*, 31 July 1992; E. Schmitt, '"People's Admiral" is Buffeted in Storm Over Ethics', *New York Times*, 1 August 1992; E. Schmitt, 'The Miltiary Has a Lot to Learn About Women', *New York Times*, 2 August 1992; 'The Tailhook Scandal', *Minerva's Bulletin Board*, 1992, pp. 5–8.

15. E. Dorn, 'Integrating the Military: Comparing the Experiences of Blacks and Women', Statement at a hearing held by the Defense Policy Panel and the Subcommittee on Military Personnel and Compensation, House Armed Services Committee, Washington, DC, 29 July 1992, p. 6.

16. Office of Inspector General, Department of Defense, Tailhook 91, Part 1 – Review of the Navy Investigations, September 1992, p. 15.

17. Ibid. p. 16. Descriptions of internal obstacles put in the way of three women soldiers who complained of assault or harassment and the conflicts of interest often denied by supervisory male officers in three different branches of the American military are included in J. Lancaster's detailed article 'In the Military Harassment Cases, His Word Outranks Hers', *The Washington Post*, 15 November 1992. This article also appears as: 'Military Macho: Harassment of Women in the Armed Services Often Means One Thing: She Asked For It', *The Washington Post National Weekly*, 23–29 November 1992, pp. 10–12.

18. For a detailed account of the intra-military debates over the defini-
tions of 'combat' and thus over where only men could serve, see
J. Hicks Stiehm, *Arms and the Enlisted Woman* (Philadelphia: Temple
University Press, 1989).
19. Some of these opinions are articulated in the 'Women in the Military' House hearings, see Note 10. They also can be found regularly
voiced in the independent but widely circulated inside the military
weeklies, *Army Times, Navy Times* and *Air Force Times*.
20. E. Schmitt, 'Many Women in Army Favor Ending Combat Ban', *New
York Times*, 11 September 1991.
21. Fuentes, 'Equality, Yes – Militarism, No', p. 517.
22. In late 1992, under the glare of media lights following the Tailhook
affair, the US Defense Department's General Counsel intiated a
review of the Pentagon's base magazine distribution policy. One
Navy commander had already unilaterally decided that his post store
would no longer carry sexually explicit literature. 'Sex-Explicit
Magazines to Face Pentagon Review', *New York Times*, 16 October
1992.
23. A. Wright, Major US Army, 'The Roles of US Army Women in
Grenada', *Minerva: Quarterly Report on Women and the Military*, 2, 2,
1984, pp. 103–113. Minerva is the best journal covering US and other
militaries' use of women. Its address is: 1101 South Arlington Ridge
Rd., #210, Arlington, VA 22202.
24. For coverage of American women in the Panama invasion: 'Women in
Arms: What Happened in Panama', *Defense Media Review*, Boston
University, 4, 1, 31 May 1990; 'Army and Air Force Women in Action
in Panama', *Minerva's Bulletin Board*, 1990; 'Combat Controversy
Destroyed Her Career, Says Linda Bray', *Minerva's Bulletin Board*, 1991.
25. C. Becraft, Women in the Military, 1980–1990, Women's Research
and Education Institute, 1700 18th Street, NW, Washington, DC
20009, 1991, p. 8. Hispanic women were 3.0 per cent of all active duty
Army enlisted women; Asian-American, Native-American and Pacific
Island women were 4.4 per cent. Together, women of colour
comprised 54 per cent of all the Army's active duty enlisted women.
By contrast, men of colour comprised only 38.1 per cent of all the
Army's active enlisted duty men. Against their 47 per cent of all
Army enlisted women, black women comprised only 19.1 per cent of
the Army's women of officer rank; all women of colour combined
likewise were under-represented in the Army's officer corps, making
up only 24.7 per cent.
26. R. Cornum, *She Went to War: The Rhonda Cornum Story* (Novato:
Presidio Press, 1992); E. Sciolino, 'Women in War: Ex-Captive Tells
of Ordeal', *New York Times*, 29 June 1992. Major Cornum expressed
similar sentiments when interviewed on NBC's 'Dateline', 21 July
1992, and on 'Fresh Air', National Public Radio, 7 August 1992.
27. I have discussed in more detail the relationships between Saudi
women's politics and American military women's politics in 'The
Gendered Gulf' in Cynthia Peters (ed.) *Collateral Damage* (Boston:
South End Press, 1991).

28.   E. Schmitt, 'Senate Votes to Remove Ban on Women as Combat Pilots', *New York Times*, 31 August 1991.

29.   Stephen Power, 'Panel on Women in Military Under Fire', *San Francisco Examiner*, 4 August 1992. I am indebted to Dan Brook for showing me this article.

30.   The recommendations of the Commission on the Assignment of Women in the Military can be obtained from the Public Affairs Office of the US Department of Defense, Washington, DC.

31.   M. R. Gordon, 'Panel Is Against Letting Women Fly in Combat', *New York Times*, 4 November 1992. Another male member of the Commission, N. N. Minow, a former chair of the Federal Communications Commission, also said afterwards that his vote in favour of ending women's exclusion from combat positions was affected in part by being the father of daughters: 'My wife and I have three daughters and three grandchildren (two are granddaughters). We do not want any of them in military combat. But ... all six are eligible someday to become president of the United States and thus commander in chief. Why should our country be deprived of the talent and commitment all six could contribute to keeping our nation safe and free?': N. N. Minow, 'Less Brawn, More Brains', *The Washington Post National Weekly Edition*, 23–29 November 1992, p. 29.

32.   Gordon, 'Panel is Against Letting Women Fly in Combat'.

33.   Ibid.

34.   See a special issue of the gay and lesbian journal *Outlook* devoted to post Gulf War commentary: 13, 1991.

6 'It Was Exactly Like the Movies!' The Media's Use of the Feminine During the Gulf War

Julie Wheelwright

A few weeks after the invasion of Kuwait, ITN 'News at Ten' from London carried an item on 26 September 1990 about 25-year-old Katherine Lambert, a British woman serving in the Gulf with the American Marines. As a lance corporal, married to a fellow officer, she and her American husband were forced to leave their four-year-old son Zach when they were assigned to Saudi Arabia in September 1990. Lambert's son was taken from their home in Hawaii to stay with his grandparents in county Durham while his parents were on active duty. On camera, a video of Lambert was played to Zach who excitedly exclaimed, 'Here's my Mummy... I kiss her lips'. Katherine was quoted as saying about her decision to join the military, 'I wanted [to do] something I wouldn't ever do in the civilian world. There are some limitations strength-wise but other than that I feel men and women are equally capable'.[1] However, British journalist Rachel Trethewey asked in a London *Daily Express* article about Lambert the following day, 'If a woman decides to have a child shouldn't she realize that concessions will have to be made in any career? Wouldn't it have been understandable four years ago if Katherine Lambert had switched to a less active part of the army?'[2] Zach was thus portrayed as yet another victim, not of war but a woman's selfish desire for professional advance.

Since television news in Britain devoted very little coverage to the issue of women in the armed forces, the ITN item was exceptional for focusing on what became known in America as the question of 'Mom's Army'. But the underlying assumption of Rachel Trethwey's rhetorical question – that women who combined soldiering with motherhood were neglecting their children – was debated on both sides of the Atlantic. The argument placed women combatants on familiar territory; since child care is still seen as primarily women's responsibility, those with a career must make concessions.[3] But the unstated emotive issue about the threat the military poses to women's inherent nuturing qualities ran deeper. 'There is a moral side to the employment of women in combat,' Field Marshal Sir Nigel Bagnall, wrote in the London *Independent*,

> For a start, men cannot bear children, nor can they replace the selfless devotion of mothers who raise the next generation. As the seventeenth century poet Thomas Otway said about women: "Nature has made thee to temper man; we had been brutes without you".[4]

American General Robert Barrow, speaking to a US magazine, appeared to concur, 'Women give life. Sustain life. Nurture life. They don't TAKE it'.[5] During the Gulf conflict, both print and television journalists often adherred to this ideology, falling back on comforting clichés.

The title for this essay – 'It was exactly like the movies!' – comes from a London newspaper interview with an American fighter pilot describing a bombing raid on Baghdad.[6] To this pilot, the devastation his weapons wrecked bore no relationship to its consequences – human death, ecological destruction or the plight of refugees. The American and British public were distanced from these aspects of the war by a heavily censored media. As media analyst Philip Taylor has argued, 'the arrangements made by the coalition for the release of information to the media during the Gulf War were in fact a highly effective form of propaganda'.[7] It was the most high-profile media war in history and the impact of censored televisual images which violated the media's own guidelines created a 'video game' effect. The quote from the American pilot refers to several significant factors which governed how the conflict was communicated to Western audiences. Servicewomen – whether as courageous supporters, brave nurses or neglectful mothers – were shown as players in this scenario of the West driving back a brutal dictator.

In attempting to understand how the war's coverage was received, it is important to remember the differences between British and American perceptions of the events. The pilot's quote was used as an ironic comment by a British journalist with the assumption that many Americans treated the conflict like an entertainment event. According to the *Independent*'s Robert Frisk, American television news, with its demands of immediacy, brevity and sound bites has become, 'the journalistic equivalent of junk-food'.[8] Many British television critics commented disparagingly on the American cable news CNN's coverage of the offensive on Bhagdad when Bernard Shaw described the saturation bombing as, 'a Fourth of July display at the Washington monument' and 'a million fire-flies'. Yet the British, according to surveys, expected their television news coverage of the war to be accurate and reliable. The greatest complaint these viewers made about the television coverage was not that it expressed bias, but that it was repetitive (43 per cent) and took up too much air time (38 per cent).[9]

It was, however, the British military authorities rather than Americans who emerged as the experts in media manipulation. American politicians, eager to overcome the 'Vietnam Syndrome' in which television was widely blamed for alienating public sympathy for the war, took up British suggestions for media control. The same model as developed during the 1982 Falklands War was applied during the Gulf conflict. In the Falklands, technical difficulties and geographical distances – the islands were 8,000 miles from home – kept most journalists far away from the action. The resulting information vacuum could be filled with the military's own experts. According to Taylor, 'what was released was invariably what each side doing the fighting and controlling the information wanted to see reach the public domain... more often than not, the media just didn't know what was happening'.[10]

Most media analysts agree that the Pentagon and the Ministry of Defence took unprecedented steps in managing the news during the Gulf War. As one postwar report described it, 'television, as it openly admitted, censored itself: scenes of human casualties in a war in which hundreds of thousands were killed, amounted to only three per cent of all its news coverage'.[11] As a rule, television is more vulnerable than print media to manipulation by state and military authorities and does not easily lend itself to analysis of complex situations. Yet according to David Morrison of Leeds University's Institute of Communications Studies, television news was the principal source of news about the war in Britain. Morrison's survey found that viewers generally expressed a high level of satisfaction with television coverage which they regarded as more neutral than the press. After analysing the survey results, Morrison concluded that the British public wants the fourth estate to become the fourth service during war. However, when faced with a 'genuine moral decision' – commitment to truth at the cost of human life – the public is not prepared to accept that journalists have the right to put professional practice first. The survey also found that it was only on the issue of saving lives that the public felt that the military was justified in suppressing information.[12]

However, such views throw the responsibility back onto the military authorities not to abuse the power they hold during armed conflicts. Yet this is a fine line to tread. During Operation Desert Shield, the Pentagon ground rules for coverage, which were condemned by several American, British and Canadian news executives, dictated that all visual images and printed stories passed through military censors. Battlefield coverage was limited to 'pool reporting' where selected correspondents witnessed the action and shared their stories with everyone else. The system, however, meant that allied commanders dictated a narrow range of issues which were covered by a few select journalists. The Toronto *Globe and Mail*'s correspondent Paul Koring noted that most accredited correspondents never left their hotels but based their reports on Pentagon briefing sessions.[13] One consequence was that the lack of 'bang-bang' (live action footage of civilian or military casualties or bombing raids), prevented an extension of the public debate about the war at home.[14] Taylor summed up this approach by stating that, 'the media were the story of this war'.[15]

Since the US Defense Department authorised fewer than 100 reporters to talk to 500,000 American servicemen and women, articles about life among the troops were also restricted. The *Detroit Free Press* correspondent described how having a 'military minder' impeded his ability to portray accurately the soldier's attitudes towards the conflict. 'You're trying to portray military people as human beings; not everybody's a hero', he told the *Washington Post*.[16] The journalists, who were placed in a 'take-me-along' position, often clad in khaki and sharing rations with the troops, adopted their own strategy of self-censorship. Those who were dependent on the televised press conferences were seen, by audiences in the US, to be 'playing into Saddam Hussein's hands' or 'probing rudely for information that's witheld for good reason' if they push the military spokesmen for answers to embarrassing or difficult topics.[17] CNN reporter Peter Arnett's coverage of the bombing of an Iraqi baby-milk factory was a case in point. His persistent questioning was condemned by several US newspaper columnists as unpatriotic.[18] In Britain, Morrison's survey of television coverage in the UK found that the British military was responsible for 13 per cent of censored material and the US military for 14 per cent. (This included restrictions on coverage by Britain's 4 terrestrial stations, the satellite channel Sky and CNN).[19]

The press was not only censored by the coalition military authorities but also by the Government of Saudi Arabia which introduced its own restrictions on reporting. New 'rules' were introduced on 18 February when access to military zones was restricted to small groups of journalists belonging to the American, British or French press pools under escort; other journalists were restricted to covering the war 60 miles from the Kuwaiti border town of Khafji. Satellite telephones – the main medium for journalists relaying their articles or 'copy' – were used only with permission from the Ministries of Information and Telecommunications specifying the type of equipment used and its location. According to *Reporters San Frontières 1992 Report*, the majority of the 1,300 specialist correspondents covering the war were prevented from doing their job under the new system and they were quick to complain.[20] Perry Kretz from the German magazine, *Stern*, noted that 'this is a United Nations War and two-thirds of the world is excluded from it'. Kretz and Adelino Gomes of the Portuguese daily, *O Globo*, organized journalists to protest against the restrictions placed on reporting during the war.

Throughout the televison coverage in Britain, women were rarely called upon as experts to comment on the conflict and are perennially under-represented as presenters and foreign correspondents. According to Morrison's study, women constituted only 8 per cent of all people interviewed in Gulf War items; they constituted only 22 per cent of all major television presenters' appearances and 13 per cent of minor presenters.[21] Interestingly, neither Taylor nor Morrison's otherwise excellent studies discuss the issue of gender dynamics in the media's coverage of the war. From the outset, then, both print and television journalists were encouraged to file reports which conformed to the military's expectations about appropriate subjects. Stories about the more than 33,000 US and 1,000 British servicewomen deployed to the Gulf reflected the military's ambivalent attitudes towards them. American servicewomen became the major focus of coverage since they vastly outnumbered their British counterparts. Since 1973 women have been integrated into all three US services where they are employed in a wider range of jobs than in the British services. But since American servicewomen had become increasingly visible in successive military campaigns in Grenada and Panama, they had generated far more media interest in Britain than their more restricted counterparts. While the Women's Royal Army Corps members attached to regiments active in Northern Ireland faced exposure to military attacks by the IRA, because of prevailing media restrictions, their role has never fitted neatly into the 'novelty' slot.

By comparison, it was not until December 1990 that the British Ministry of Defence decided to disband the WRAC and integrate its members into previously all-male regiments. The majority of British servicewomen deployed to the Gulf were medical personnel, administrators, Territorial Army medics and, for the first time, 20 Women's Royal Naval Service personnel served aboard a naval ship, the *HMS Brilliant*.[22] But this was not simply a numbers game. Since the British media were largely harkening back to coverage of the Falklands War, in which no servicewomen participated, there was no precedent for covering the story from this angle. In recent history, however, British journalists, along with their American counterparts, had devoted many column inches to the debates raging about the US servicewomen's active participation in similar military interventions in Grenada and Panama.

So it was the American woman in Marine fatigues, packing her gun under the desert sky who became the *British* media's stock image of the female warrior. Newspapers in the UK thus skillfully projected unquestioned assumptions about how their culture evaluates female autonomy by drawing on 'orientalist' assumptions. If, according to this still-pervasive ideology, all Arab women are dehumanized within Arab culture, American women are 'liberated' to a ridiculous degree. The London *Evening Standard*'s Washington correspondent, Jeremy Campbell, wrote after the peace was declared, 'in warfare in which the nature of the front line is increasingly blurred, those wider opportunities [for women] have become much more dangerous'.[23]

The first stories emerging in the British press from the Gulf, after the deployment of a 50,000 strong US task force in August, juxtaposed the novelty of the white, Western female soldier against the shrouded Saudi woman – a visual comment on the presumed 'backwardness' of Arab cultures. The servicewomen were then rapidly elevated into harbingers of a new dawn for Saudi womanhood. Sgt Sherry L. Callahan, a 25-year-old, told a *New York Times* reporter what she and other Army women felt on arriving in Saudi. 'At first we were angry. We were deployed here to save these people and, like, they don't want us because we're women'.[24] American journalist Laura Flanders linked the women soldiers more directly with an ethnocentric theme of liberation. As she wrote, 'Not only are there [Kuwaiti] women victims to be rescued, there are also women soldiers who can demonstrate the superiority of the American way through contrast with their oppressed Arab sisters'.[25]

The presumption of American egalitarianism extended to reports that Saudi soldiers' initial hostility to the US servicewomen had given way to more enlightened attitudes. The British press also carried reports about these tensions and, on 17 August, the *Daily Mail* ran a full-page feature on the 'feminine face of conflict in the Gulf', reporting on the 'culture shock from America's soldier girls in the kingdom of the cover-up'. Saudi ground crews were reportedly angry that servicewomen had stripped down to t-shirts while working on fighter jets in the fierce heat. Again, the US women were portrayed as leading nothing short of a self-conscious crusade to change conditions within Saudi, even if only on a restricted army base. The attitudes of the Saudi men were not given and neither were their objections contextualized to provide background to this particular conflict. The press therefore reported the Saudis as expressing a sexist ideology which, by implication, had been eradicated from the American military leadership. 'Saudi ideas about women', the servicewomen had been assured, 'would not disrupt military operations'.[26] Although the Pentagon was exercising practical considerations rather than ideological concessions to sexual equality in deploying servicewomen, the sympathy lay with the 'soldier girls' as extensions of male fighting units. In this instance, considerations of race had overcome those of gender.

On the same page, the *Mail* carried a report from an un-named correspondent on '36-year-old mother-of-two', Maryam Rajavi, who was described as 'the youngest general in Saddam Hussein's army [who] claims to have killed 30,000 enemies and takes no prisoners because they are too expensive to feed'.[27] Rajavi, who had fled from Iran with her husband because of their opposition to Khomeni's Government, formed a Mujahadin army which includes a contingent of women soldiers. The *Mail* report claimed that Rajavi views Western women as 'too soft' while her own female recruits drill for three hours a day, abstain from sexual relationships and eat frugally. Yet in contrast to the photograph of American staff sergeant, a very feminine April Hanley, Rajavi is described as a latter-day Amazon: 'With her Kalashnikov assault rifle and a belt of hand grenades, and dressed in olive-green fatigues and khaki headscarf, she has no pretensions to femininity. "I am not interested in such things", she says'.[28] The two accompanying photographs of Rajavi holding her gun and looking meek in a chador carry the caption, 'Iraq's women soldiers are ruthless and willing to die for their country.'

The contrast between the two images of the women combatants is striking and informed as much by issues of politics and race as they are by gender. In this report, militarism is conflated with liberation for the US servicewomen yet when Rajavi's women soldiers trade their chadors for Kalashnikovs, the transformation unsexes them. The report takes Rajavi's extravagant claims at face value and attributes her female troops with a rapacious killer instinct. The Arab women, through the *Mail*'s eyes, cannot grasp the meaning of liberation: they swing wildly from passivity to guerilla action without the steadying hand of liberal democracy. However, as I will discuss later on, the US servicewomen's media value often serves only as a foil for other issues. In this case, the barbarity of Rajavi's aims is assumed without attempting to understand the particular circumstances in which her military involvement and those of her female troops has evolved.

Another striking example of the 'liberation' theme was reflected in several reports about the Riyadh car strike. In November, the *Times, Guardian, Financial Times* and *Independent* reported the Saudi women's protest against a long-standing ban on female drivers. Forty-nine veiled women – all professionals – drove through downtown Riyadh in convoy as part of a wider equal rights campaign in Saudi.[29] One woman interviewed in the *Independent* said that the protesters were inspired by witnessing Kuwaiti women refugees driving cars across the border and by US servicewomen in trucks. According to these press reports, the Government's response to the protest – the ban was enshrined in law – appeared as an indirect criticism of the servicewomen rather than a tactic in internal Saudi politics.

The history and context of the struggle for women's rights in the Middle East was ignored in this equation as journalists speculated on the Western servicewomen's influence. For example the support that these women received from groups such as Egypt's Arab Women's Solidarity Union, or Aicha in Algeria, was never mentioned. The British and American press reports also overlooked the importance that *Kuwaiti* female drivers had on Saudi women. 'I [was] thrilled to hear that Kuwaiti women, who are allowed to drive and go unveiled, were even driving down our roads and into the streets of our capital', commented one Riyadh resident.[30]

As an indication of how important this event was in challenging the Saudi Government's position on women's civil rights, Salih al Azzaz, editor of the monthly *Tejarat al-Riyad* and regional reporter for the Arabic-language monthly, *Al-Majalla*, published in London, was arrested on 19 November 1990 for photographing the demonstration and for alerting the foreign press to it. Azzaz was held without charge for four months.[31]

The stories which appeared in the Western press, however, indirectly placed the US military in a highly flattering light as an institution promoting equality. Internal conflicts and ambiguities about integration such as sexual harassment, fraternization and inadequate career advancement, were rarely linked to the female soldier's day-to-day experience.[32] Yet these issues have been central to arguments over the past 20 years that women in combat zones would upset military discipline and preparedness. When issues of gender were discussed in US news reports, concerns about – as Cynthia Enloe has described it – 'womenandchildren', reflected a distinct ethnic bias.[33] Western servicewomen and hostages received the highest news ratings while the dilemmas of Filipina domestic workers, Sudanese migrant labourers or Bedouin women were relegated to background news shots or articles on the war's incidental consequences. In sharp contrast to the concern for the Westerners held hostage before their release, a report that 116 Indian nurses had disappeared from Baghdad hospitals where they were working, and were possibly being held captive in Iraq, warranted only a few lines in the quality press.[34] Their rights were not news.

The 'liberation' stories inadvertently raised the public profile of US servicewomen and increased the Pentagon's support for their deployment. As recently as 1990, a survey of American women by a national women's magazine voted 'military officer' onto the '10 worst careers list'.[35] Recognizing that military service sits uneasily with those constituencies which are usually supportive of women in non-traditional occupations, Pentagon officials were undoubtedly conscious of the servicewomen's media profile. The focus on female combatants as 'Moms' eased anxiety about their 'masculine' role while attaching the conflict to an issue with which most American working women can identify. Iraqi women, by contrast, were portrayed in highly compartmentalized roles. Although Maryam Rajavi's name was prefixed with 'mother of two', she was not questioned about the conflict she might feel between her political commitments and her work. But the refugees and few television shots of Iraqi civilian casualties focused almost exclusively on 'womenandchildren'. Again, the Western woman, struggling to combine these roles, served as a measure against which the 'underdevelopment' of gender relations in the Middle East could be understood.

However, even concerns about servicewomen were inconsistent in terms of their news value. In mid-December several articles in the British press reported on the military's efforts to provide entertainment to combat the loneliness and frustration their military personnel were experiencing in the Gulf. Despite living under the same exacting conditions as their male colleagues, their emotional needs had neither been addressed nor recognized. Both the British and American press reported that the US Embassy had hired three women strippers from a Bournemouth agency for Christmas shows aboard the English *Cunard Princess* for US troops in Bahrain. The agency's owner, Dave Woodbury, said the strippers would either tone down the show down or perform before an all-male audience. On a phone-in to a Washington DC television show after news about the strippers broke, Woodbury said he was confronted with wives and girlfriends who were concerned about the atmosphere aboard ship. He defended the performance by stating, 'Striptease, whether you like it or not, is big business in this country. It's very acceptable and good entertainment for the boys who've been working hard out there'.[36] While none of the British papers mentioned the subsequent protest by family groups, one Washington newspaper quoted Caroline Sparks, president of the Feminist Institute in Bethesda, as saying that the strippers' performance would worsen a difficult situation for servicewomen, who had already begun to file complaints about sexual harassment.[37]

The emphasis on using erotic shows to keep 'the boys' happy became a popular theme in the Western press. On 27 January Reuters revealed that military censors had suppressed as 'too embarassing', a *Washington Post* report that Navy pilots watched pornographic films before a bombing mission into Iraq.[38]

However, the British tabloid press, which prides itself on its jingoistic appeal, equated this form of entertainment with patriotism. *The Sport* ran a sexual advice column for 'our boys in the Gulf', and arranged pornograhic pen-pals for them. 'We are all pretty pissed-off cos booze is banned and all the women here are totally covered up', wrote Sapper Partlow, 37 Field Squadron, BFPO.[39] *The Sport* claimed to have received 'sackfuls' of such letters, requesting correspondents, pornographic calendars and back issues of their newspaper.

Despite the servicewomen's significant presence, news stories concerning the soldiers' rest and recreation invariably focused on how the men were coping with imposed abstinence. On 26 January both the *Guardian* and the *Independent* carried reports that shares in Okamoto Industries, Japan's largest condom manufacturer, had risen because of rumour that Allied soldiers were using these prophylactics to 'keep sand out of their gun barrels'.[40] A spokesman for LRC Products, the manufacturers of Durex, confirmed that the Ministry of Defence had ordered half a million sand-coloured condoms.[41] To reassure the public that this was not a 'blind', signaling an escalation in sexual activity, the MoD also confirmed that throughout the conflict contraceptives were passed out by medical staff and were equally available to servicewomen. An MoD press release further stated that, 'soldiers are strictly instructed to observe local customs and stay away from Saudi women folk and to do otherwise would cause serious offence to our allies and damage relations with Saudi Arabia'.

While the majority of British servicemen were posted 'far from temptation' and warned against relations with 'Saudi women folk', the military also enforced a rigorous no-fraternization rule within the services. But when a WRNS (Women's Royal Naval Service) officer and a Royal Navy helicopter observer were caught kneeling naked on a bunk aboard *HMS Brilliant*, the Navy's 'no touching' policy was given a different meaning in the press. There was a sense of relief expressed in British reports about the episode: while heterosexual relations between service personnel would be punished, at least male soldiers were not breaking other sexual taboos. Later, John Costello, author of *Love, Sex and War*, suggested that the US and British military might be

considering guidelines for dealing with 'Emergency Homosexuality', a term for same-sex relations during wartime.[42]

The twin concerns of homosexuality occurring in the
absence of sexually available women and inter-service affairs
were obliquely addressed in the press. The incident aboard
the *Brilliant* was considered particularly important since it
was the first Royal Naval Warship to carry 'Wrens' and 14
were deployed during the Gulf War. The announcement in
1990 that 'Wrens' would be allowed to sail aboard Naval
ships met with resistance from a group of Navy wives who
protested in the ports of Plymouth and Portsmouth that it
would lead to extra-marital affairs. The *Brilliant* crew were,
therefore, under close scrutiny. A diary item in the *Evening
Standard*, however, claimed the incident between Sub-
Lieutenant Jacqueline Ramsay and Lieutenant Mark Davies,
was 'a red-blooded, heterosexual yarn whose only drawback is
that the penalties paid by both parties... reflect the way that
differences in rank still matter more to the senior service
than equality of sex'. Diarist Alexander Walker, who in-
correctly identified Ramsay's rank as 'stewardess', finally had
evidence of the soldier's sexuality in the Gulf being exercised
in an appropriate manner. While the infantry soldiers might
be poring over pornographic letters orchestrated by the *Sun*,
officers were having sexual relations with their professional
equals. The consequence of the courts martial that followed,
however, affected the officers differently. Despite Sub-Lt
Ramsay's statement that she and helicopter observer Mark
Davies had not engaged in sexual intercourse, Lt Commander
Penny Melville-Brown, defending, said notoriety would follow
her throughout her career.[43] Although Davies, who flew 30
combat missions during the war and was considered a Gulf
hero, was sent home in disgrace, his career remained intact.

Male soldiers' notions of masculine privilege were strengthened by this public and official attention to their perceived
need for objectified sexuality. A British MoD spokesman said
Saudi objections had cancelled 'blue shows' and bare-
breasted Page Three girls which are regular forms of entertainment. The response of servicewomen was completely
absent from these press reports, along with any mention of
sexual harassment. But on a symbolic level, whether they were

soldiers, prostitutes or entertainers, women still represented the human face of war. A *Guardian* report on 26 January about British Air Force mechanics described their tradition of painting pornographic female figures onto fighter bombers. The planes had become women to be cajoled, bullied or punished, but above all controlled, by the mechanics who could therefore distance themselves from the reality of the bombers' purpose.[44] Thus the new focus on servicewomen did not counter the equation between militarism and masculinity.

Press reports about the welfare of US servicewomen were often directly connected to the function they served as feminine mascots. This became immediately apparent when 20-year-old Army Specialist Melissa Rathbun-Nealy went missing in action during the Battle of Khafji on 31 January. The British tabloid newspaper *Today* ran a banner headline on its front page, 'The Unthinkable of War: Girl GI Taken by Iraqi Snatch Squad' and quoted a senior American officer as saying, 'a woman POW is the ultimate nightmare'. The jingoistic *Sun* also put the story on page one with the headline, 'At the Mercy of the Beast' and stated that 'Allied military chiefs think the Iraqis – who treat their OWN women appallingly – might abuse or even rape the captive' (emphasis in original). Under the paper's flag, the newspaper urged its readers to pray for 'the girl Marine, may God protect her'.

While the *Sun*'s support for the war had included urging British women to knit 'willy-warmers' (for the male soldier's genitals), its writers now piously mourned the fate of Rathbun-Nealy. The very real concerns about the sexual torture a female POW (prisoner of war) might face, however, were background to the political function that such a tragic situation could serve as war propaganda. As the *Sun* report indicates, the major concern was that Rathbun-Nealy would be treated like an *Iraqi* woman and therefore harmed or degraded. Although the situation was entirely new to the press – the only previous American women taken as POWs were nurses – its fears were steeped in familar rhetoric. From the First World War onwards, the definition of rape as a crime against women in most Western European countries has depended on the context in which it occured. Rape has been considered historically a spoil of war and therefore, notoriously difficult to punish.

Ironically, Rathbun-Nealy was statistically much more likely to have been sexually harassed by her fellow soldiers than attacked by her Iraqi captors. A Pentagon survey released in September 1990, after Operation Desert Shield had already begun, suggested that the majority of US servicewomen were subjected to sexual harassment, despite efforts to banish discrimination from the services. A large majority – 64 per cent – of the 9,497 American military women surveyed the previous year said they had been harassed in some form, ranging from derisive whistles and jokes to suggestive looks and sexual assault. (Five per cent reported they had been raped or sexually assaulted.) The survey ordered in 1988 followed scathing reports that nearly all of 220,000 women in US forces were subjected to discrimination and harassment.[45] The month following the Pentagon report, the US Navy acknowledged that it had a major problem with rape, sexual assaults and violations of 'fraternization' rules in its training centres. Yet only one out of the 13 cases of sexual assault reported at the training centre in Orlando, Florida, resulted in court-martial proceedings.[46]

In fact, it was not until July 1992 that the true extent of sexual harassment that female servicewomen experienced during the Gulf War came to the media's attention. During the Senate Veterans Affairs Committee hearings Army Specialist Jaqueline Oritz described being 'forcibly sodomised' by her sergeant in broad daylight on 19 January 1991. Oritz, who was an Army mechanic and the only woman in Delta Company of the 52nd Engineer Battalion, says she immediately reported the attack to her superiors but 'unfortunately, my claim fell upon deaf ears'.[47] Army Specialist Barbara Franco told the committee that she was raped by three soldiers at knifepoint during basic training while two other women complained that male superior officers dismissed their reports of sexual assault. As Senator Dennis DeConcini commented after the hearings, 'American women serving in the Gulf were in greater danger of being sexually assaulted by our own troops than by the enemy.' The Senate hearings also followed the resignation of the US Navy Secretary Lawrence Garrett, over revelations that more than 26 women, including 14 officers, were run through a gauntlet of men who abused them at the annual 'Tailhook' meeting of Navy aviators.[48]

Even during the Gulf War there were hints from American servicewomen that sexual harassment could become a major problem. 'There were hard stares and harder hits', a woman signaller told a *Newsweek* reporter in August 1991. 'Some guys hadn't seen a woman for five months and they acted like animals... They assumed we were [already] doing it.'[49]

Despite the well-documented evidence that American servicemen are frequently disrespectful of their female colleagues' sexual autonomy, press reports that included this aspect in their analysis of the furor surrounding Rathbun-Nealy's capture were rare.[50] According to Susan Brownmiller, author of *Against Our Will* (1975), while there was extensive press and television coverage of the female POWs, the US public 'are very reluctant to believe our guys would ever rape a woman'.[51] Given the pressure to portray the soldiers in a positive light and the presence of military censors, I found no contemporary reports that challenged this belief. Instead much was made of the 'clean war' where soldiers had no access to drugs, alcohol or prostitution.

Without this analysis, the spectre of a US servicewoman being raped easily became another indictment of Hussein's regime and a crime which belonged exclusively to the enemy. The American military's own very poor record on the rapes committed by servicemen in Vietnam appeared to have been completely forgotten. Throughout the Vietnam War, the incidence of rape was so high that a 'double-veteran' became a common slang among American soldiers: 'Having sex with a woman and then killing her made one a double veteran'.[52] Taken in this light, the 'US source' who claimed to be worried about Rathbun-Nealy because of 'the reputation of the Iraqis' begins to look very different. In reality, neither side could claim moral superiority in its treatment of women as either soldiers or civilians.

When Rathbun-Nealy was released, however, the attention her plight had commanded in the press appeared to have afforded her a degree of protection. Her father Leo Rathbun told the press in Newaygo, Michigan, after speaking with his daughter in Saudi Arabia, that except for being beaten by an Iraqi soldier in a transport truck when she was first captured, she was well treated by her captors. She had described the Iraqis who held her for more than a month as 'absolutely beautiful people' who had taken excellent care of her.[53] Her greatest fear came during the Allied bombing raids on Baghdad when the force of a blast once threw her across the room. The only suggestion that she had been threatened during her captivity came when an Iraqi asked to drink a whisky with her. She turned him down but according to her father Leo, 'she did smoke a cigarette with him'.[54] Leo added that his daughter's Iraqi captors considered her a 'beautiful hero' who they compared to Brooke Shields and Sylvester Stallone. This intriguing pastiche of masculine and feminine images, however, also indicates the exceptional status Rathbun-Nealy gained as a captive. She was treated like a Hollywood film star, not a prisoner of war.[55]

Yet even after the conflict had ended, the US Administration stressed the ordeal of her captivity. In August a Bush Administration official at a Washington press conference reported that the two women POWs – Rathbun-Nealy and Major Rhonda Cornum – were *both* sexually threatened and one was fondled by her captors. The Department of Defense officials added only that 'neither was raped'.[56] While not denying the difficulty both women must have endured as captives, the Defense Department's insistence on the abuse Rathbun-Nealy suffered appears at odds with her own statements. Once again, the issue of women's sexuality played an important role in the lexicon of wartime propaganda. When Rathbun-Nealy was captured, her military role was instantly collapsed into her gender. It was presumed that as an *American woman*, she was far more significant to the Western media than as a soldier.

Nowhere, however, was the nexus between masculinity and soldiering more apparent than in news articles which dealt with motherhood. The televised scenes of American mothers leaving young children at home as they boarded ships for the Gulf became a staple image. (A British equivalent appeared not to exist, possibly because there were only two reported cases of couples being deployed together and none of women refusing because of parenting.[57]) The American military more accurately reflects the national percentage of single mothers at 16 per cent among its 82,000 female members. But by January 1991 fewer than 100 women had been granted parental discharges and two mothers, who were forced to leave the Army because they could not find child care, fought for honourable discharges.[58] According to the US Defense Department, children from 17,500 families were left without the custodial single parent or without both parents and about 16,300 single parents were deployed.[59]

The press focus on small children as uncomprehending victims of war, who blamed their soldier-mothers rather than fathers, both parents or even inflexible military policy. In fact, there are more single fathers – unmarried or divorced military men with children – than military women. (However, the majority of divorced fathers do not retain custody of the children and this issue is often used by the Pentagon to blur the problem that single mothers face). According to Carolyn Becraft, director of a project on the military for the Women's Equity League, opponents of expanded roles for women seized on the parenthood issue because other arguments had been debunked in the Gulf. 'This whole issue is about power and whether women will be allowed to displace men in high-ranking positions', she told *The New York Times*.[60] But from September 1990 the press had dubbed the conflict a 'Mom's War' because of the number of mothers deployed.

A survey of American newspapers' coverage of service-women's role during the war supports this narrow interpretation. The University of Southern California's 'Women, Men and Media' project analysed the representation of women in several newspapers including the *New York Times,* the *Los Angeles Times,* and the *Chicago Tribune*. The analysts found that while 85 per cent of front-page news was devoted to the activities of male soldiers, articles about servicewomen almost exclusively addressed their family and marital status:

The great majority of stories focused on men – their jobs, their weaponry, their opinions. There were few stories about women soldiers and those that did appear were centered on the women's parental status. Female soldiers were seldom quoted and photographs of women were mostly of them at home showing concern for absent family members. Editorials and news stories about the war's impact on families were critical of mothers for going to war, and expressed concern about the effect on children. There were no articles or editorials on the impact of a father leaving his children published during the study. A photograph of Army Captain JoAnn Conley with a badge picture of her daughter affixed to her helmet was widely circulated, but there were no photographs showing men with pictures or mementoes of their children. There were almost no photographs of women with weapons or performing their duties. A series of articles was devoted to what male soldiers carried to the front to remind them of home – primarily women's underwear. The few female soldiers interviewed said they carried pictures of their partners or families[61]

There are a number of significant issues which arise from the way in which this conflict was presented. Philip Schlesinger, Professor of Film and Media Studies at Stirling University, has noted that national audiences want television news to reflect their own society, designed to allow them to become involved in the issues covered.[62] So the ITN News item focusing on Katherine Lambert rather than *both parents* being separated from their son because of professional commitments, had a resonance for British viewers. Despite the heralding of the New Man's involvement with his children – a potent upmarket advertising image – parenting within the military's masculine context was still shown as an exclusively female responsibility.

Moreover, pregnancy was portrayed as a nuisance, and a deterrent to military preparedness, just as civilian employers might view it as a hindrance to business efficiency. Reports about the 36 pregnant crew members aboard the destroyer tender *Acadia* in late April, earned it the derisive label, 'Love Boat' and a Navy report stated that 'pregnancy is viewed as epidemic'.[63] However, in a postwar assessment of women's participation, Colonel David H. Hackworth found that many servicewomen complained bitterly that their units 'kept exacting statistics on pregnancy but not on men's sports injuries'. Col. Robert Poole, the physician heading the triage centre at Andrews Air Force Base confirmed that sports injuries actually produced the largest number of casualties in the Gulf.[64] In addition, pregnancy rates among servicewomen were actually comparable to rates among civilian women in the 20–24 age group and among military women during peacetime.[65]

Yet rumours persisted that servicewomen used their pregnancy to gain preferential treatment and, in autumn 1991, a Navy study reported 'a perception' among male and female sailors that 'some enlisted women became pregnant primarily to get out of sea duty or an unpleasant situation'.[66] A *Washington Times* article in September 1990 also claimed that four of the 22 women in the 360th Transportation Company scheduled to leave for the Gulf were found to be pregnant; all had conceived less than six days before their regiment was deployed. However, Carolyn Becraft dismissed critics who claimed these soldiers became pregnant to avoid the call-up, adding that women in the military receive only six weeks maternity leave.[67] In Britain, when a 'Wren' got pregnant, presumably on shore leave, it was reported in the *Daily Mirror* with the headline, 'Navy Wren Wendy Clay's actions during the Gulf War weren't what England expected – she became pregnant'. However, there was no mention of the fact that her fiancé was also a sailor aboard HMS *Brilliant*.[68]

Nightly television reports in the US showing servicewomen working in a variety of jobs 'normalized' their presence over several months according to Pete Williams, Secretary of State spokesman. He commented afterwards that, 'One of the lessons we've learned from Operation Desert Storm is the extent to which the nation accepted the significant role of women in that operation'.[69] Although the American House Armed Services Committee has recently approved an amendment permitting the Air Force and Navy to use women pilots to fly combat missions, a recent survey suggests that their role as mothers is still perceived as a problem by the public at least.[70] A *Newsweek* poll conducted on 25 and 26 July 1991 found that while 53 per cent of respondents supported women in the armed forces getting combat assignments if they want them, 89 per cent would worry about mothers leaving small children at home and 76 per cent feared pregnant women would put the fetus at risk.[71] The military is left grappling with inherently contradictory aims: it needs well-educated women recruits but attempts to preserve its masculinist ideology by refusing to accommodate family needs.

The Gulf War, where five American women died in combat, two were captured and 33,000 served along with 1,000 British servicewomen, has highlighted the extent of women's military involvement. However, given the press restrictions, correspondents rarely challenged assumptions about the role women played in the conflict. As we have just seen, the image of the gun-toting woman Marine was used to condemn Arab oppression without placing either women's struggle within an appropriate political or historical context. Although servicewomen were portrayed as enjoying sexual equality, military officials gave priority to the emotional needs of their male counterparts. Finally, pregnancy among servicewomen was another strong indicator of the military's ambiguous attitudes towards women's complete integration.

Despite the emphasis on women soldiers as a novelty, they are not new to either the British or American armed services. In both countries, female combatants have unofficially served since the eighteenth century and have always provided an extensive network of auxiliary services.[72] However, press coverage of servicewomen's role during the Gulf War focused on precisely those anxieties about sexual equality which mark contemporary Western societies. The war became a crucible for questions of women's relationship to real economic, social and political power, and revealed how remote the goal of equality remains.

Notes

1. ITN 'News at Ten', 26 September 1990.
2. R. Trethewey, 'Should a Mother go to War?', *Daily Express*, 27 September 1990.
3. An American poll in 1984 found that 40 per cent of women said their husbands shared equally in child care; two years later, the same poll

found only 31 per cent of women still agreed with this statement. S. Faludi, 'Blame it on Feminism', *Mother Jones*, September/October 1991.

4. 'A Call to Arms in the Battle of the Sexes', *Independent*, 12 August 1991.
5. D. G. McNeil, Jr., 'Should Women Be Sent in to Combat?', *The New York Times*, 21 July 1991.
6. 'Sound Bites', *The Guardian*, 19 January 1991.
7. P. M. Taylor, *War and the Media: Propaganda and Persuasion in the Gulf War*, (Manchester University Press, 1992) p. 25.
8. G. Henry, 'A Credibility War that TV News Won', *Guardian*, 20 January 1992.
9. D. E. Morrison, *Television and the Gulf War*, (London: John Libbey, 1992) p. 6.
10. Taylor, *War and the Media*, pp.13–14.
11. Morrison, *Television and the Gulf War*, p. 6.
12. Ibid.
13. P. Koring, *Globe and Mail*, 24 January 1991.
14. *Detroit News*, 17 January 1991.
15. Taylor, *War and the Media*, p. 15.
16. *Washington Post*, 11 February 1991.
17. 'Combat and Combative Reporters', *New York Times*, 1 February 1991.
18. For analysis of the 'baby milk plant episode', see Taylor, *War and the Media*, pp. 111–118.
19. Morrison, *Television and the Gulf War*, p. 74.
20. *Reporters Sans Frontières 1992 Report*, (London: John Libbey, 1992) p. 178.
21. Morrison, *Television and the Gulf War*, p. 69.
22. Interview with Ministry of Defence (MoD) spokesman, 8 November 1991.
23. J. Campbell, 'Why Did So Many Army Women Die?', *Evening Standard*, 6 March 1991.
24. *New York Times*, 25 September 1990.
25. L. Flanders quoted in 'Women and the Gulf War', Church Women United, New York, NY, 1991.
26. Ibid.
27. 'West Stuns East in the Sun Baked Desert', *Daily Mail*, 17 August 1990.
28. Ibid.
29. D. Sharrock, 'Women Take a Back Seat as Driving Ban becomes Law', *The Guardian*, 15 November 1990.
30. J. P. Sasson, *Princess*, (New York: Doubleday, 1992) p. 204.
31. *Reporters Sans Frontières*, p. 178.
32. *Washington Times*, 12 September 1990, carried a Reuters story about a recent Pentagon survey suggesting that a majority of women in the US military were subjected to sexual harassment. According to

the *New York Times*, 26 May 1991, 'in the Gulf, the Army said it investigated 11 allegations of indecent assaults, seven cases of sodomy, two attempted rapes and one of adultery involving female personnel'.

33. C. Enloe, 'Women and children', *Village Voice*, 25 September 1990.
34. *Independent*, 26 January 1991.
35. Reported in *European Stars and Stripes*, 25 July 1990.
36. Interview with author, 20 January 1991.
37. *Washington Times*, 8 January 1991.
38. 'US Censors porn-film reports', *Independent*, 27 January 1991.
39. 'With Love and Kisses from Fiona', *The Sport*, 30 January 1991.
40. 'Desert Shield', *Guardian*, 26 January 1991.
41. J. Wheelwright, 'The Sexual Heat of Battle', *Guardian*, 31 January 1991.
42. Conversation with author, 28 January 1991.
43. A. Walker, 'Navy Larks', *Evening Standard*, 19 March 1991 and 'Navy Pair Pay Price of Liaison', *Guardian*, 14 June 1991.
44. D. Sharrock, 'Nikkie and the Fairies Keep Spirits High with the RAF', *The Guardian*, 26 January 1991.
45. *Washington Times*, 12 September 1990.
46. *Washington Post*, 22 October 1990.
47. E. Sciolino, *New York Times*, 1 July 1992. See also Susan Thom Loubet, 'A Soldier's Story', *Ms*, November/December 1992, p. 88.
48. M. Walker, 'Sex Attacks "rife" on US Servicewomen', *Guardian*, 2 July 1992.
49. *Newsweek*, 5 August 1991.
50. J. Wheelwright, 'The Hidden Horrors of War', *Guardian*, 18 February 1991.
51. Conversation with author, 1 February 1991.
52. Quoted in C. Enloe, *Does Khaki Become You? The Militarization of Women's Lives* (London: Pluto, 1983) p. 34.
53. E. Walsh, 'As Brave as Stallone... Beautiful as Brooke Shields', *Washington Post*, 6 March 1991.
54. *Evening Standard*, 6 March 1991.
55. See also K. Muir, *Arms and the Woman* (London: Sinclair-Stevenson, 1992) p. 30.
56. M. Healy, 'Pentagon Says Iraqis Tortured or Abused All US POWs', *International Herald Tribune*, 3–4 August 1991.
57. C. Bolland, Women's Royal Army Corps, interview with author, 20 January 1991.
58. 'Women and the Gulf War' (see Note 25) p. 10 and J. Wheelwright, 'Mothers of the Battle', *Guardian*, 24 January 1991.
59. 'Pentagon Details Cost to Children', *Washington Post* Service, 16 January 1991.
60. J. Nordheimer, 'Women's Role in Combat: The War Resumes', *The New York Times*, 26 May 1991.
61. Muir, *Arms and the Woman*, p. 179.
62. 'The Media Show', Channel Four, 15 August 1990.

63. Col. D. H. Hackworth, 'War and the Second Sex', *Newsweek*, 5 August 1991.
64. Ibid.
65. Nordheimer, 'Women's Role in Combat'.
66. Ibid.
67. J. Wheelwright, *Amazons and Military Maids: Women Who Dressed as Men in Pursuit of Life, Liberty and Happiness* (London: Pandora, 1989).
68. *Daily Mirror*, 30 September 1991.
69. M. Moore, 'Women at War, or How Gulf Brought the Debate Up Front', *International Herald Tribune*, 7 May 1991.
70. P. Towell and E. Palmer, 'Women of War', *CQ*, 11 May 1991.
71. Hackworth, *War and the Second Sex*.
72. Wheelwright, *Amazons and Military Maids*.

Part III
Case Studies

7 The Militarization of Woman and 'Feminism' in Libya[1]
Maria Graeff-Wassink

Modern Libya has been little studied, and is known almost exclusively for its negative aspects. Although typically Mediterranean in climate and Maghrebin in population, language and culture, it is a country that differs greatly from its neighbours. Does its marginalization derive from its colonial past (for a whole generation it underwent Italian Fascism), or from the present regime, whose peculiar features are generally perceived in negative terms? Those two phenomena are probably linked.

The Libyan institutions broadly reflect this position. Libya is, for instance, the only country in the Arab world where there is military service for girls and a Women's Military Academy (WMA). In a regime generally presented more as fundamentalist than modernist, these original features of aggressive feminism are at first confusing. The WMA, when it was set up in 1979, was indeed in open contrast with the customs and traditions of this patriarchal country. That led one to suspect that it might constitute something different from just one more military institution, training a few hundred extra officers per year.

Our study began in 1985, with a series of interviews with representative samples of Women's Academy pupils and staff. This research ended by confirming that the Academy was indeed a truly 'symbolic' institution, with as its objective nothing short of training a new female élite intended to embody not only the military woman but above all 'liberated' Libya (liberated from the yoke of the patriarchate). The function of the Academy's pupils is to act as a model and an example for all women, not only in Libya but also abroad. The point was accordingly to provoke, to shock, to create a precedent in a society still very patriarchal and traditional. It was at the same time to upset the image women had of themselves with the object of giving them confidence in themselves.

The Libyan woman, especially in towns, traditionally lived in seclusion, not leaving home except on rare occasions, and in that case invariably veiled from head to foot and accompanied by a man of the family. It is true that for years, even at the times of the monarchy, there had been attempts to improve their position. But the laws in that connection were of little use as long as the mentality of the women – and the men – did not change. Legislation aimed at improving women's status had accordingly not brought any notable changes. Girls had, it is true, begun to attend school – education became compulsory for them. But from the moment of puberty their fathers took them away, to shut them up at home as tradition desired. All their education was in any case aimed at securing their future as mother and wife, subject to a man's will.

1. THE REVOLUTION

Immediately on gaining power in 1969, the revolutionary group showed its ambition to change the country, modernizing it and creating a new model of society. In the endeavour to offer a version of Islam that would be at the same time fundamentalist and progressive, Libya has sought constantly to reconcile the values of progress with a certain respect for tradition. Woman's emancipation is fitted into this original, general and overall context of the reorganization of society. Thus, in deciding to use women as a lever of social change, the object was accordingly not only to improve their condition but to bring about a transformation of society as a whole, through a change in mentality, of all mentalities, both of men and of women.

2. THE INTRODUCTION OF NEW STRATEGIES

These ambitious proposals called for recourse to new strategies. The first step was the introduction of compulsory military service for girls. This obligation was not very well received by fathers, be it clear. For three successive years the proposal was rejected by the 'General Congress of the People'. The arguments put forward were many and varied. Gheddafi recalled that in the tradition of Libya there had already been calls upon women in war in the past: 'From the palanquin carrying her, a woman would accompany the men in war, encouraging them and inciting them to fight.' He also recalled that in the history of Libya women had often played the part of 'women under arms'. Had the example not, moreover, been given by the entourage of the Prophet? Ayesha, his favourite wife, had had a not only political but also military role (personally leading an army). Thus tradition, history and religion showed that the militarization of the Arab and Moslem woman was not a novelty, but in harmony with Libyan society as it ever was, in profound accord with its values.

The argument that was ultimately to convince the General Congress was, however, one of a political nature: the threat of American imperialism, or more exactly American-Israeli. Parallels were then drawn between the then Libya and Israel, where women were already taking part in defence, to conclude that Libya, too, with the same number of inhabitants, had the same need to mobilize all forces in its own defence. War, too, was in any case no longer solely a matter for men: the whole population was potentially a victim, since bombs drew no distinctions between men and women. The law on enlistment of women was promulgated in 1977, eight years after the 'Free Officers' came to power. It concerned only girls; married women were exempt. Thenceforth, girls at puberty, instead of remaining shut up in the home stuffing themselves with sweetmeats, were to put on uniforms to do the physical exercises of military training.

3. CREATION OF THE WOMEN'S MILITARY ACADEMY (WMA)

The opening in 1979 of a Military Academy reserved for women was a second step in this feminist strategy. On the occasion Colonel Gheddafi stated:

Women will not be free or respected or exercise their rights until they are strong and have taken possession of all the weapons: firearms just like the weapons of science, knowledge, culture and revolution. Women's entry to the Army will constitute the move to a new strategic stage, a qualitative leap.

He went on to clarify:

Only a limited number of girls will enter the WMA, since not all are suitable for becoming officers. These military aspirants must be in good condition of health, have an outstanding personality and be educated. A degree, even from a university, is not sufficient: it is on personality, competence and general culture that a woman soldier or officer will be judged, and it is only if she has those qualities that she can manage to impose herself on the men and on soldiers. Only in this way can she attain to military honours, be in the vanguard of a 'armed people' and be an example to all women.

Accordingly, though destined for training the élite cadres of the 'woman under arms', the WMA had also, and especially, the implicit function of creating a new guiding image for all women – Libyan, Arab and other.

4.   MOTIVATIONS IMPELLING PUPILS TO A MILITARY CAREER

Logically, the selection of candidates for this career ought to be based not only on physical and intellectual criteria, but also on what the WMA staff defines as 'comprehension of the ideas of the revolution'. Consequently, the impulses and motivations impelling young Libyan women to undertake a military career are different, at least in part, from the usual ones. One does, admittedly, find the traditional motives like a taste for order and organization, *esprit de corps* and comradeliness, a sense of responsibility and attraction for the uniform, or even others of a universal nature like identification with a male model (a military father or brother). But the majority of our sample explain their professional option with arguments that seem directly inspired by revolutionary ideology and Libya's specific situation. Over two-thirds of those interviewed motivated their entry to the WMA by revolutionary and ideological convictions:

> The Colonel has opened all doors to women. If woman is to have the same place as man in society, she must be able to participate in defence too, and if necessary in war.

> Libya was a poor, oppressed country, which the revolution has freed; we, the young generation, wish to take part in the revolution of which we are the first beneficiaries.

> We have the duty to defend the conquests of the revolution.

To justify the need for women to know how to defend themselves, allusions are often made to the Middle Eastern situation: 'Events in Lebanon have shown how necessary it is to know how to defend oneself; there all the women were able to do was weep and mourn'.

Given the specific nature of these motivations, becoming a soldier seems for these young women to constitute more an act of militancy than the pure and simple adoption of a new occupational environment. Being part of the Army and participating in the defence of one's country represents, over and above an individual achievement and a professional career option, a personal contribution to the social progress of the Jamahiriya (the 'State of the masses'). At bottom, they have a twofold vocation: to incarnate the new woman (the 'liberated woman') and to be the future cadres of the 'People's Army'. What, then, is their conception of the 'liberated woman'? What does the 'People's Army' mean for them?

5. THE LIBERATED WOMAN

To answer the first question, there are three characteristics most frequently cited:

1. Sense of responsibility: they emphasize that they acknowledge the limits (physical, moral and religious) of the
   freedoms they claim;
2. Liberation from prejudices and from 'what others will
   say'; – equality with man ('She must participate in all the
   country's activities, political, social and economic –
   within the limits of her own physical powers');
3. Open mentality ('She must be an educated woman, open
   to new things, to science, always in touch with what is
   going on in the world').

In sum, the liberated woman as perceived by the officer
cadets, is freed from the tutelage of man, open to the progress and evolution of society; she is a responsible person
demanding to be treated as an adult, that is on an equal foot-
ing, and hence a citizen in every respect.

6.   THE PEOPLE'S ARMY

For some fifteen years, Libya maintained a duality in its own
military system. On the one hand was a classical Army, in-
herited from the monarchy, from which the 'Free Officers'
too had come; on the other was an Army called 'the People's',
imbued with the spirit of the revolution. The concept of
militarization of women was introduced in 1975 as a corollary
to the creation of the 'People's Army'. The point was to apply
the ideology of equality, the axiom underlying participation
of women in the life of the nation. From 1974, the theme of
'direct democracy' had been introduced into political life and
had given rise to a whole series of structural reforms. The
conception of active, direct participation by all citizens in the
progress of the country is at the root of the introduction of
general military training and of the creation of the People's
Army (from which women were excluded until 1977). With
the official proclamation of the Jamahiriya in September
1977, the concept of a people under arms was clarified in the
following terms: 'In the Jamahiriya, weapons are no longer a
monopoly of the classical Army. Weapons are now in the
hands of all citizens, male and female. Bearing arms is a

right and duty of every Libyan woman' (1978 speech by Gheddafi). The concept of a people under arms was aimed not only at defence against external aggression; it was also to play an internal function, 'defence of the revolution by the armed popular masses'. An Army colonel gave us the following explanation in this connection:

> The Libya of the Jamahiriya lives under a permanent threat because of the ideas and the options of the revolution. This threat comes principally from outside, but also exists within the country, represented for instance by the fundamentalist Islamic policy that does not accept our ideas, particularly in relation to the emancipation of women.

The role of the career Army becomes essentially technical, aimed at organization, incorporation into the hierarchy and training. The People's Army and the classical Army lived side by side for 14 years; co-existence was often difficult, and at times openly conflictual. The slow transformation of the military organization was officially completed only in 1988, with the suppression of the classical Army. But according to our enquiry, in the mind of the young generation the duality of the institutions had already ceased to exist: 'We, career soldiers, keep our rank in the People's Army and become its professional specialists.'

7. HOW WOMEN OFFICERS SEE THE PEOPLE'S ARMY

How is the People's Army perceived by women officers? One of our interviewees put it like this:

> If we had not created the people under arms, there would not have been any women soldiers in Libya. The woman under arms is a conquest of the people under arms. In other countries women do not have our same position in the army, even at the same rank. In France a woman colonel is the result of a technical career in the army. Here, it is the result of a struggle for the people's power. If we want the people to govern itself, it is necessary for it also to be armed.

This profession of faith corresponds, according to the survey data, with the opinion of the majority of WMA officer cadets.

8. OPINIONS OF THE MILITARY

But are their male colleagues of the same opinion? How do they accept the intrusion of women into a sphere that had belonged to them alone? What is their image of the military woman?

Our survey done in 1989 (ten years after the entry of the first women officers to the Army), on a sample of 50 male officer cadets, shows that their image of the military woman is far from being negative: 59 per cent of those questioned were entirely favourable to women's participation in the Army; around half of them thought they were also able to take part in front-line fighting. 32 per cent hesitated and gave qualified answers, weighing up the pros and cons; only 9 per cent were entirely opposed to the entry of women to the Army.

An analysis of the qualifying adjectives used in relation to military women supplies useful clarification. Two categories may be distinguished in the vocabulary used. On the one hand are the adjectives of approval: the military women are described as 'open, free, educated, proud, strong, strong-willed, responsible'. These terms are antonyms of those used by the interviewees to define the 'traditional' women: 'uneducated, ignorant, submissive, dependent, treated like an object, reclusive, non-participant'. Otherwise, recourse to a number of 'technical' words makes more direct reference to the military status: 'punctual, model soldier, respectful to superiors, able to secure respect, exemplary, intelligent at work, a real specialist'.

The first category of adjectives clearly reflects assessment of the military woman as a 'liberated' woman, while the second category refers to military status. While the Libyan military woman seems well accepted by the majority as a 'comrade', she is much less so as a possible partner. Only 5 per cent would prefer to marry a military colleague, while 43 per cent hoped to avoid such a marriage. It should be noted, however, that for half those interviewed 'a military or a civilian woman are the same thing'. As for the qualities attributed to a military woman in her role as wife and mother, one-third of the answers indicated doubt as to these: a civilian wife would offer more guarantees in this connection.

A breakdown by age shows a positive correlation: the younger (under 24) are more favourable than the older (24–30) to militarization of women. It is interesting to note that there is not by contrast any correlation with social background (measured by father's educational level).

9. OPINIONS OF OTHER GROUPS

From a series of group discussions in various social contexts in Tripoli in 1986, it emerges that seven years after its creation the Women's Military Academy was already on the whole well accepted. Conversely, there was often criticism of the fact that the WMA was a boarding institution, because 'a girl ought to live with her parents until marriage'; boarding does not in fact fit Libyan tradition or usage.

How was this society, still so traditionalist, able so rapidly to accustom itself to such a revolutionary and feminist idea as the militarization of women? After all, the topic is still an object of much polemic in the West itself!

It seems that the answer as far as Libya is concerned has to be sought in a set of different but convergent causes: the Libyan past, the Islamic conception of war, the regional political situation, and not least the special nature of Libyan feminism – a type of feminism introduced from above and in part thanks to the military themselves. Women have been offered a place equivalent to men's, along with the right to widespread participation. The official rhetoric has imposed on the Army, especially its cadres, a certain sort of feminist comportment. Opportunism and conformism have done the rest, without forgetting the importance of the experience of work in common as a factor in changing stereotypes.

10. CONCLUSION

Colonel Gheddafi's regime has for over 20 years been seeking to replace the ancestral Libyan patriarchate, shut up in an orthodox, traditionalist Islamic context, with new models of relationships, and to promote more fraternal, egalitarian values. Both theory and practice are aimed at systematically introducing into society a radical change in mentalities, through initiatives ranging from legislative provisions to measures aimed at promoting the emergence of new feminine models.

The creation of a Women's Military Academy is to be interpreted against this background. In striking contrast with the country's customs and traditions, the WMA was from the outset aimed at accelerating the process of modernization. The woman under arms, a symbol of the 'liberated' woman in the sense of being an adult able to defend herself by herself, is to be a model for all women. The military identity does not accordingly diminish her feminine identity.

On the other hand, the need for security and defence has further legitimated her role. This is a need directly associated in Libya with the political struggle and the fight to make the ideological choices triumph: 'Protecting the conquests of the revolution', as they say. Among these conquests is women's participation in political decisions, making her a citizen to all effects. Thus the Libyan woman, whose model is the military woman, has become a sort of accomplice of power, alternately vehicle and agent of the new ideology.

With opening the Army to women, their role, like men's, had necessarily to change, since the two things are strictly linked. The entry of women into the Libyan Army has, moreover, been facilitated by the fact that it was not a rigid, male-dominated structure, but an institution in rapid evolution, gradually being transformed from a classical professional Army to a sort of crucible where, by definition, participation of women was to strengthen the merger of all citizens aimed at creating and stabilizing a 'State of the masses' (Jamahiriya).

Revolutionary Libya has accordingly sought to change the image of the Army, and consequently of war. The Libyan Army is regarded as a popular institution, a political instrument in the service of all citizens and in support of an ideological choice. Accordingly, becoming one of the cadres in this People's Army may be presented as an honour and a social and political promotion for both women and men. The observations I have made tend to show the existence of a close connection between collective psychological needs and the evolution of social structures. The acceptance of women's militarization by the Libyan collectivity is one example.

It further follows from this analysis that it is hazardous to draw comparisons between institutions taken out of context. Comparisons of this type (between one military academy and another, in one country or another) call for much caution, for they risk leading to erroneous conclusions. The same thing would be true of anyone seeking to reduce the image of the Libyan woman under arms to the partial, restrictive one of the Colonel's famous bodyguards. Great account has to be taken of the historical and sociological differences which, at the level of collective psychology, determine the specific nature of individual mentalities. Current research in this sphere ought to take account of this fundamental fact in order not to create false impressions that prevent an understanding of the reality and of the truth itself.

Appendix

The Women's Military Academy, Tripoli

The Women's Military Academy (WMA) was inaugurated on 2 February 1979. It offers Libyan – or Arab, representing some 10 per cent of total numbers – girls a training at two levels:, from the third year of secondary school, six months' training as a soldier; from the sixth, i.e. last, year of secondary school, two years' training as an officer. The admission conditions are, apart from educational level, age (between 17 and 25), nationality (Libyan or Arab), father's authorization, satisfactory physical condition and good understanding of the ideas of the revolution.

The officer cadets sign a five-year commitment. They can study for the school-leaving certificate (science or arts), if they do not yet have it, or in the afternoon follow university courses in Tripoli in a faculty of their choice. For their second year of study, officer cadets must choose among four specializations: administration, information, communication or defence. Trainee soldiers may further specialize in music and join the women's military band. The WMA programme includes on the one hand military training and on the other theoretical courses. The programme is the same as at the Men's Military Academy (MMA), except for a few exercises regarded as too violent for women (hand-to-hand combat, etc.). Some courses are done jointly with pupils of the other Academy; the same is true for major manoeuvres outside town.

Today the instructors are in the main women (WMA alumni); this staff is to be feminized still further. Since last year the vice principal too has been a woman. The teachers of theoretical subjects come from outside: most of them are university professors (men and women) and soldiers (MMA teachers). Pupils board at the Academy throughout the school year.

Officer cadets may according to their education choose, after taking the diploma, from among three different continuations:

1. Specialization in one of the higher military academies (Navy or Air Force), which since 1981 have also taken in women;
2. Securing a cadre posting in the WMA itself, with a possibility of continuing university studies they have started;
3. Joining a military unit, preferably located in their city of origin, in which case they may live at home.

As far as women soldiers are concerned, after their six-month diploma the majority go for military training courses in high schools or in centres reserved for married women volunteers. In its 13 years of existence, the WMA has trained some 2,000 officers and a little over 3,500 women soldiers. According to statements by the cadre staff (teaching and medical) the failure percentage is minimal (from 1 to 2 per cent).

All military ranks are open to women: their careers are the same as those of all professional soldiers. The same is true of pay (in Libya salaries are in general equal for women and men). In September 1992 around 100 women officers from the first intake (1979) who had continued a military career secured the rank of commander. This is at present the highest rank Academy alumni have reached; accordingly there are not yet (1993) any women colonels in the Libyan Army.

Note

1. This article summarizes the results of field research conducted by the author in Libya and described extensively in her book, *Les femmes en armes. Kadhafi féministe?* (Paris: Armand Colin, 1990). This book was published in English by Darf Publishers Ltd, London, in December 1993.

8 Penelope's Web: Female Military Service in Italy – Debates and Draft Proposals, 1945–92[1]

Virgilio Ilari

1. THE ABSENCE OF MILITARY WOMEN IN ITALY AND CONSCRIPTION

The absence of female personnel in the Italian Army constitutes one of its conspicuous anomalies in comparison with Western military models. But this anomaly is only the consequence of another anomaly, namely the relatively low percentage of career or voluntary personnel by comparison with conscripts. It should be recalled that in Western armed forces female recruitment is exclusively voluntary in nature (even for the proportion enlisted only for the national service period), and conscription of women is the practice only in countries in exceptional situations.

It should also be noted that, apart from ideological or legal motivations, *de facto* recruitment of women (voluntary and/or compulsory) always derives from a quantitative or (more frequently) qualitative shortfall in the male quota: the qualitative deficit may also derive from political, ethnic or racial causes. It may be felt preferable to give weapons (or open professions or political careers) to women, as long as they are, say, middle class, supporters of the party in power, white, or Jewish, rather than to men who do not offer such loyalty guarantees: the women warriors of Dahomey or President Gheddafi's bodyguard, Israeli recruits, South African volunteers, etc.

But in European and Western armies, the qualitative deficit of the male conscript intake in turn originates both on the

150

labour market and in economic development, bringing about feminization of occupations no longer appealing to skilled male personnel.

In modern armies, occupations of a logistical, technical or administrative nature are requiring increasingly higher levels of education and qualification; moreover, they predominate over combat roles in diversification and specialization, in percentage of personnel and in educational qualifications required for admission to competition. Moreover, in Western societies the armed forces (and to a lesser extent the police) have some difficulty in competing with public or private employers.

Apart from military 'vocations' (in any case limited, even among officers), the average level of education and qualification of enlisted males (especially among volunteer troops and NCOs) is often lower than the national average for the labour force.

In professional or highly professionalized armies it is possible, in order to handle combat tasks with male personnel, to extend recruitment increasingly to the modern proletariat constituted by ethnic or social minorities (including noncitizens and foreign mercenaries, which in any case do not represent more than, for instance, one-third of the professionalized regiments in the French armed forces). But to handle the more specialized tasks, it is increasingly necessary to have recourse to female personnel.

However, in armed forces with large numbers of conscripts available, the case appears very different. These recruits furnish the army with educational and occupational qualifications and mental elasticity that it would be hard to find in the average volunteer (including women), at a price of not even, in the Italian case, a sixth of that of a volunteer – at least from the viewpoint of salary alone.

In Western armed forces, at least to date, military women (including many officers) have almost exclusively been assigned tasks that can without difficulty be handled by redraftees, by reserve officers, former officers or NCOs (noncommissioned officers), or civilian workers or employees. In Italy this labour is in surplus supply. By contrast with professional or semi-professional armies, the Italian Army has had no real need to extend recruitment to women. It has often been recognized that recruitment of women could have improved the choice and ensured the planned numbers in this or that category of career personnel; but these advantages always seemed very marginal by comparison with the drawbacks (financial, psychological, technical, etc.) of recruiting women.

2. THE DISCIPLINING OF EQUALITY, OR 'FROM LEGAL EXCLUSION TO ADMINISTRATIVE EXCLUSION'

Even though (since 1925) bound to the 'sacred' duty of defending the country, Italian women are even today exempt from compulsory military service.

The origin of this exemption goes back to the law on conscription and recruitment (today in Article 1 of Presidential Decree no. 237 of 14 February 1964), which until 1986 made only 'male citizens' subject to conscription. In the new formulation contained in Article 1 of Law no. 958 of 24 December 1986, the adjective has been dropped, so that by the letter of the law citizens of the female sex are at present also subject to conscription; in fact military service has continued to apply only to male citizens. Not only has nothing changed in practice and in the regulations; the change has not even been noted in the debate on women's military service.

Like any other exemption from military service, women's forms part of the restrictions on the military obligations the ordinary law may lay down pursuant to Article 52 of the Constitution ('Military service is compulsory within the limits and in the manner laid down by law'). In principle, then, conscription could be extended to women through an ordinary law, with no need to amend the Constitution.

Despite this, the armed forces refrain from making use not only of conscription but even of enlistment, whether voluntary or through public competitions (according to the different categories of personnel). Neither the law nor competition notices explicitly reserve voluntary enlistment or participation in competitions to citizens subject to conscription. One might indeed maintain that these forms of recruitment are mutually independent, deducing this from the fact that the minimum age for voluntary enlistment or participation in certain types of competition is lower than the conscription age (16 instead of 18).

In consequence, the exclusion of women from voluntary enlistment and from military careers is not, in Italian legislation, founded on exemption from conscription. On what legal norm is it based, then?

Law no. 1176 of 17 July 1919 and the regulations approved by Royal Decree no. 39 of 4 January 1920 barred to women a large number of public employments, including those connected with military defence of the state: that is, all employments in the 'military services and corps of the Royal Army and the Royal Navy' and in the police corps.

Nonetheless, in 1948 the Constitution of the Republic laid down the principle of equality between the sexes: moreover, Article 51 explicitly laid down the right of access to public offices for 'citizens of both sexes... on terms of equality, in accordance with the qualifications required by law'.

Despite this, no less than 15 years of debate and many opinions from the Constitutional Court were needed (among them no. 33 of 18 May 1960 declaring Article 7 of Law 1175/1919 'unconstitutional') in order for Article 51 of the Constitution to be finally implemented.

Thus, Law no. 66 of 9 February 1963 abrogated the 1919 law and the 1920 regulations and allowed women into 'all public offices, professions and employments, including the magistracy, in the various roles, careers and categories, without restrictions in relation to duties or career advancement except for the qualifications required by law'.

Parliament rejected an amendment proposed by the government aimed at excluding women from employment in the armed forces or from civilian employment in support of operational or logistic units. Nonetheless, Article 1 of the law left the regulation on women's service in the Army, and in what the text in an unaccustomed legal formulation calls 'special corps', to future 'particular laws'.

But to date, that is, some 28 years after the 1963 law, the only 'particular laws' concerning women in uniform remain those relating to the police forces.

In 1959 a small corps of women police was in fact created, with auxiliary powers. It was only after the demilitarization of the police in 1981 that women were admitted without restriction to the same roles and careers as male police. In ten years, this has led to very marked feminization of the state police: in 1992 women were some 10 per cent of the numbers, but have been as many as 60 per cent of constables, inspectors and officials recruited since 1986. This feminization has declined recently, but only thanks to various expedients and indirect discriminations, such as the reservation of enlistment quotas to males who have already done their own compulsory military service in the police.

Since 1990, women have also been allowed into the prison service, the state forestry corps and the fire brigade, in each case with full equality of careers and duties.

We must however ask whether a 'particular law' was really necessary in order to open the military career to women, or whether it might not be done simply administratively, since ultimately, after the 1919 law had been declared unconstitutional, that is since 1960, there was no longer any law in being in the Italian legal order barring women from admission to competitions for recruiting career military personnel.

Undoubtedly, the lack of the 'particular law' provided for by Article 1 of the 1963 law led to a phenomenon of self-exclusion by Italian women. Of course, every so often a dozen or so girls submit applications for admission to the military competitions, the notices of which do not either explicitly or indirectly exclude citizens of the female sex. But in almost the totality of cases, the women candidates have not appealed to administrative justice against the rejection of their applications by the military administration: the latter referred, somewhat hypocritically, to the above-mentioned Article 1, as if the 1963 law could *de facto* surreptitiously relegitimate the old discrimination it had itself abrogated, in compliance with the Constitutional Court ruling.

On only one occasion, in 1981–82, did one of the candidates, Diadora Bussani, go the full length of the administrative channels against her rejection by the defence administration. The Tuscany Regional Appeals Tribunal (TAR), in Ruling no. 482 of 15 October 1981, accepted the appeal of the young Triestine Diadora Bussani against exclusion from the competition for the Leghorn Naval Academy. The TAR verdict was, however, quashed by the Council of State, in judgment no. 526 of 28 July 1982.

Bussani subsequently secured a condemnation of the state from the Court of Justice of the European Communities, and the symbolic satisfaction of honorary enlistment in the US Navy, conferred on her on 2 November 1982 by the Commander of the *Mount Baker*, an auxiliary vessel in the Sixth Fleet.

In accord with the majority of legal scholars, the TAR had interpreted Constitution Article 51 as a further, more detailed, specification of the principle of equality laid down in Article 3, though denying that it gave the ordinary legislature the power to circumscribe it or derogate from it. Consequently, the interpretation of Article 1(2) of Law 66/63 as a (necessarily unconstitutional) derogation from Article 1(1) could not be accepted. According to the TAR, it should instead be interpreted as a mere programmatic norm with no sense of precluding exercise of the right by citizens of the female sex to undertake a military career, which could be regulated by the legislature, but not voided by its failure to act.

The Council of State's grounds were by contrast the provision of special norms on enlistment of female personnel made by Article 1(2) of Law 66/63, interpreted as a derogation from the provisions of Article 1(1). The constitutionality of this interpretation was based on the assumption that Article 51, in specific relation to admission to public offices, had left to the ordinary legislature the specification of the operative requirements of the equality principle laid down in Article 3, invoked by the appellant: these requisites for suitability might legitimately also include sex, as recognized by Constitutional Court judgment no. 56/1958.

Without adding force to these technical arguments, sufficient in themselves, the judgment went on to note that 'for employment in the armed forces',

> direct relevance [might be assumed] by such physical factors as muscular strength or resistance to fatigue and pain, but also, and particularly, character traits like

resistance to shock and capacity to conquer fear, as well as even qualities that in normal circumstances are regarded as negative, like the instinct to overpower and the capacity to injure and kill other human beings.

Although, as we noted above, the Court of Justice in The Hague had condemned the Italian state to reimburse damages, Diadora Bussani was unable to pursue her military dream.

We must acknowledge the Council of State's exquisite love of country, reaching as far as the extreme sacrifice of not only law but even logic, in order to defend the masculine integrity of the Italian armed forces: in essence, it found that in the specifically military sphere, sex could as such be regarded as a 'quality required by law', in accordance with the restriction on the equality principle in access to public employment accepted by Article 51 of the Constitution.

Accordingly, pending the 'particular law' promised since 1963, the exclusion of women from military competitions was held not to be unconstitutional.

After the sigh of relief for the Council of State's heroic verdict in the Bussani case, which as Emanuele Rossi commented 'took the [government's] chestnuts out of the fire', the spotlight turned away from the question of female military service.

3.   POLICE REFORM

In fact it appeared increasingly difficult to secure passage of a measure which would regulate access by women by limiting it to some and not all military careers. There was, moreover, the precedent of the police reform recently approved (Law no. 121 of 1 April 1981), where Christian Democratic amendments aimed at introducing a 20 per cent 'quota' had been rejected. It was said at the time that the quota, apart from being unconstitutional and in any case unfair, was also otiose because female police candidates would be self-selecting. It was later seen when (after 1983) the first enlistments on the basis of the new law began to come, that women represented around 40 per cent of applicants but no less than 55 to 70 per cent of those passing, since for a multiplicity of social and cultural reasons an occupation traditionally disdained by more skilled men seemed desirable to women of the same level. In less than a decade this brought about (despite subterfuges and expedients of every sort aimed at reducing the number of female competitors, such as increasing the minimum height) a rate of feminization quite out of line with those in foreign police forces where there are quotas and limitations on such employment. While in leading and intermediate roles (commissioners and inspectors) the matter did not offer any great drawbacks other than those of a psychological and socio-cultural nature for the new female image that resulted, and indeed offered the advantage of better selection, the case was different for lower ranks, employed on tasks where physical performance and resistance were of relevance, if only in enhancing deterrence and making it less necessary to have recourse to arms, and where mixing might have negative effects on the service. Despite the pragmatic triumphalism, there are a few indications that in reality things were rather different. In any case, it is easy to suppose that the lower average performance by female personnel is one of the reasons impelling the inflation of staffs, with growing financial burdens; while one wonders what might happen once male personnel enlisted before the reform are withdrawn from operational tasks for age reasons, and only the increasingly slender male intakes of later enlistments can be used to form mixed patrols.

It might, with some basis, be supposed that just this uncontrolled feminization of the police might have counselled prudence in opening military careers to women. There would be no risk or drawback had the opening remained within the limits of the government decree law. Nor, however, would there be any guarantee against ideological maximalism and radical leaps forward in parliament. The political sectors and pressure groups those might have come from, which even had they wanted to could not have escaped the duty of calling for them if only not to deny their own internal logic, for the moment covered things up by making the principles of anti-militarism and pacifism take precedence over that of equality. Moderates and the Right, who had blandly sponsored female military service as lip-service to the principle of equality, in reality seemed delighted to be able occasionally to exhibit their own proposed laws on the rare occasions where that seemed to offer some advantage. As for the administration, apart from a few officers or officials in love with the idea, there really did not seem any enthusiasm to see it realized.

There remained, to be sure, the women directly concerned. But apart from a few cases, there were no signs that solid military vocations were compelling to young Italian woman-hood, and if there were they could better be directed towards the police, where in any case there were many more oppor-tunities to use weapons than in the armed forces of a peace-ful country like Italy. Had military enlistment been open to women, the female proportion of the boundless hoards of systematic competition entrants would certainly have grasped that opportunity, too, as it had done in the case of the police. But as long as it remained closed, there was little likelihood of seeing them on poster parades beneath the windows of Palazzo Baracchini.

Appendix

Thirty-one years after the declaration of unconstitutionality of the law excluding women from military employment, there are still no women soldiers in Italy.

On the other hand, the technical studies and draft laws presented have by contrast been numerous, but all expired since it was not possible for both Houses of Parliament to discuss them before the end of the legislative terms.

The basic chronology is like this:

1943–45: the Italian Social Republic created a Women's Auxil-iary Service (SAF) with 6,000 members, while the Kingdom in the south created a Women's Auxiliary Corps (CAF), with 400 volunteers, with civilian status, dissolved in 1946.

1947: the Constituent Assembly rejected amendments to the future Article 52 aimed at excluding women from compuls-ory military service, leaving the restriction to ordinary laws.

1967: after several years' drafting, a Defence GHQ working group set up to study recruitment of women completed a technical study by proposing a solution similar to the one then in force in the United States and Britain, namely the creation of a special auxiliary service with specific regulations and careers.

1974: draft laws by the Democrazia Cristiana (DC), in government since 1935 and Movimento Social Italiano – Destra Nazionale (MSI-DN), a neo-fascist party: the first in this connection both provided for insertion of female personnel into a specific corps or auxiliary service (it should be stressed that in 1974 in the United States women's auxiliary corps had been dissolved and the personnel taken into normal roles, though with restrictions on combat use).

1976–77: Draft laws by PSDI (Partito Social-Democratico Italiano) (1976) and MSI-DN (1977) providing for a women's auxiliary service.

1977: defence White Paper (1977): for the first time provided for entry of women soldiers into male roles, though excluding combat commissions, and consequently the highest-skilled posts.

1979: the Accame bill provided for 50 per cent of military postings to be reserved for women.

1980: a CASD study confirmed the GHQ policy providing for acceptance of women into corps and into technical, logistical and administrative roles in the armed forces, always excluding combat roles.

1981: the Lagorio Bill (during the Spadolini Government): the Government's first bill, tabled two days after the ruling by the Tuscany TAR in favour of Bussani, and evidently directed at displaying the Government's commitment, though with no real intention of translating it into action.

1981: Law no. 121 of 1 April: the reform of the police, including admission of women. The limitations on employment permitted by the law were all suppressed in practice: parliament rejected a proposal to set a percentage 'ceiling' on enlistment of female personnel.

1982: Council of State judgment on the Bussani case (7 June).

1985: Defence White Paper.

1986: Savio-Scaiola etc. Bill (A.C. no. 4022, 1 October 1986): single Women's Corps.

1986: Spadolini Bill (A.S. no. 2016, 31 October 1986), identical to the Lagorio Bill: admission to competition for recruitment of officers and NCOs in technical, logistic and administrative roles and commissions, excluding combat roles and use.

1986: opinion of the National Commission on the achievement of equality between man and woman (under the Prime Minister), chaired by Socialist Elena Marinucci, on the Spadolini Bill (9 December 1986): though having the suspicion that women's military service was aimed not at equality but more at resolving the shortage of male personnel, in essence the opinion was in favour of the bill, though criticizing, without too much insistence, the exclusion of combat roles, regarded as a source of limitation on career opportunities. It should be stressed that this last comment denotes the Commission's ignorance of the norms concerning the organization of military personnel, since career progression to the rank of general was separately regulated in each of the roles that might have been open to women. The opinion given by the 'house feminists' denoted a division in the Italian feminist movement, which was borne of left-wing movements and had thitherto been opposed to women's military service on grounds of principle or ideology: pacifism, anti-militarism, the specific nature of female culture. For the first time, defence of 'equality' won as against pacifism and anti-militarism.

1987: On 21 January the Senate Defence Committee began consideration of the Government and MSI-DN bills on women's military service. For the first time the media seriously considered the problem, something customarily dealt with only as a curiosity, in summer. Opinion polls showed a majority in favour.

1989: January. Costa Bill (DC): more or less like the Government Bill.

1989: 16 November. Meeting and debate on women's military service organized by the CESPEURO (socialist women).

1989–90: Women's military service and voluntary admission of women to civilian national service (to be introduced in place of compulsory military service) are provided for by a number of bills in connection with reform or abolition of compulsory military service, and with voluntary recruitment.

October 1992: first experiment, to a purely propagandistic extent, in opening the armed forces to women: 29 girls selected among those who had applied for admission to the competitions to recruit officers or NCOs were given hospitality, for less than 48 hours, in the Roman barracks of the 'Lancieri di Montebello' and put through psychological tests at the end of the 'experiment', much highlighted by the mass media (though accompanied by many criticisms and reservations, not only from left-wing women's movements but also from popular magazines).

November 1992: provision for enlistment of women (excluding combat roles and, for the first time, provision for a percentage 'ceiling') incorporated in the bill from Defence Minister Salvo Andò providing for semi-professionalization of the Italian armed forces and a drastic reduction in the conscription proportion to one-fifth of the age group.

Note

1. For a complete bibliography on secondary and primary juridical sources, see V. Ilari, *Storia del servizio militare in Italia*, v, 2 (Rome: Riv. Militare, 1992), pp. 389–423 (*La difesa della patria, 1945–1991*), pp. 427–30 (*La questione del servizio militare femminile*).

Bibliography

This bibliography chiefly treats the topics dealt with in this volume: accordingly, it refers mainly to the theme of women in the armed forces, not to that of women in war (in civilian and/or military roles).

The need to distinguish the two areas (a distinction sometimes not possible, as in the case of the Gulf War) arises from a number of considerations: (1) This volume does not contain articles of a historical nature on women's experiences during warfare; (2) the area of studies of women in conflicts is, along with that of women and pacifism, the most developed and hence oldest; accordingly, the bibliographies cited at the outset, for instance the one annexed to E. Isaksson's book, are able to supply excellent indications here; (3) moreover, the area closest to us, namely women in contemporary armed forces, is a very recent area of interest, in continuing evolution. This is primarily a result of the mere fact that it is only recently that women have been fully accepted into the armed forces (and in fact not into all of them), so that the interest of female scholars (many of them themselves military women) and male scholars was attracted only after the second half of the 1970s. This means that as far as this specific area is concerned bibliographies require continual updating, and the last ten years have represented a period rich in fundamental contributions on the theme, seen from the twofold perspective described in the introduction (the viewpoint of women and the viewpoint of the institution). Demonstrating the increased interest in this area of research, in 1982 in the United States, at the behest of Linda Grant De Pauw, a quarterly review (*Minerva*) was created, entirely dedicated, as the sub-title 'Quarterly Report on Women and the Military' indicates, to issues concerned with women and the military system. The late 1980s also saw deeper consideration of one central theme of the debate this volume indirectly deals with: the relationship between armed forces and society. This bibliography takes account of that too.

In view of the usefullness of continuously updating the appropriate bibliographical tools on such a broad theme as women and war as such (in the threefold sense of women and military institutions, women and conflicts, women and pacifism), we wished in this bibliography to introduce, apart from the works cited in the articles and those on women in the armed forces, a few classics dealing with women and conflicts and women and pacifism, with particular reference to the English-language literature.

It should finally be recalled that, unless cited in the text, this bibliography shows neither unpublished articles nor those produced by special services under government auspices (for American ones, refer to the bibliography edited by J. H. Stiehm in 1989).

BIBLIOGRAPHIES AND GUIDES TO THE ARCHIVES

Annotated Bibliography, in R. R. Pierson (ed.) *'They're still Women after All'*: *The Second World War and Canadian Womanhood* (Toronto: McClelland and Stewart, 1986).

Bibliographical Essay, in N. Goldman (ed.) *Female Soldiers. Combatants or Noncombatants? Historical and Contemporary Perspective* (Westport: Greenwood Press, 1982).

Bibliography, in E. Isaksson, *Women and the Military System* (New York: Harvester-Wheatsheaf, 1987).

Bibliography, in J. H. Stiehm, *Arms and the Enlisted Woman* (Philadelphia: Temple University Press, 1989).

'Bibliography of Journal articles published in English between 1980 and 1990', *Journal of Women's History*, 3 (1991) pp. 141–58.

Cambridge Women's Peace Collective (ed.) *My Country is the Whole World*: *An Anthology of Women's Work on Peace and War* (London: Pandora, 1984).

Dunn, J. P., 'Women and the Vietnam War: a Bibliographic Review', *Journal of American Culture* (1989) Spring, pp. 79–86.

Palmer Seeley, C., *American Women and the US Armed Forces. A Guide to the Records of Military Agencies in the National Archives Relating to American Women* (Washington: National Archives Record Administration, 1992).

'Women in the Military: An Annotated Bibliography', *Armed Forces and Society*, special issue on 'Women as New "Manpower"', 4 (1978) pp. 695–716.

Women in the Military: A Selective Bibliography (Washington: Pentagon Library, 1983).

BOOKS

Aït Sabbah, F., *La femme dans l'inconscient musulman* (Paris: Albin Michel, 1986).

Albrecht-Heide, A. and U. Bujewski, *Militärdienst für Frauen?* (Frankfurt a.M.: Campus Verlag, 1982).

Anderson, K., *Wartime Women: Sex Roles, Family Relations and the Status of Women During World War II* (Westport: Greenwood, 1981).

Aron, R., *La société industrielle et la guerre* (Paris: Plon, 1959).

Assembly of Western European Union, *Report: The Role of Women in the Armed Forces*, Baarveld-Schlaman (rapporteur) (Paris: 1991).

Baker, M., *NAM: The Vietnam War in the Words of Men and Women Who Fought There* (New York: Morrow, 1981).

Ballweg, J. A. and Li Li, *Military Women: Problems, Stress, and Health Concerns* (Blacksburn: Women's Research Institution, 1990).

Battistelli, F., *Marte e Mercurio. Sociologia dell'organizzazione militare* (Milan: Angeli, 1990).

Beard, M., *Women as Force in History* (New York: Collier, 1972).

Berkin, C. and C. Lovett (eds.) *Women, War and Revolution* (New York: Holmes and Meier, 1980).

Berube, A., *Coming Out Under Fire* (New York: Plume/Penguin, 1991).

Binkin, M., *Military Technology and Defense Manpower* (Washington DC: The Brookings Institution, 1986).

Binkin, M. and S. Bach, *Women and the Military* (Washington DC: The Brookings Institution, 1977).

Braybon, G. and P. Summerfield (eds) *Out of the Cage, Women's Experiences* in *Two World Wars* (London: Pandora, 1987).

Brownmiller, S., *Against Our Will* (New York: Bantam, 1976).

Buck, J. and L. Korb, *Military Leadership* (Beverly Hills: Sage, 1981).

Caire, R., *La femme militaire des origines a nos jours* (Paris: Lavauzelle, 1981).

Callaway, H. and R. Ridd (eds) *Caught up in Conflict: Women's Responses to Political Strife* (London: Macmillan, 1986).

Campbell, D'A., *Women at War with America: Private Lives in a Patriotic Era* (Cambridge, Mass.: Harvard University Press, 1984).

Cassin-Scott, J., *Women at War, 1939–1945* (London: Osprey, 1981).

Chapkis, W., *Loaded questions: Women in the Military* (Amsterdam and Washington: Transnational Institute, 1981).

Clark, I., *Waging War: A Philosophical Introduction* (Oxford: Clarendon, 1990).

Cleaver, T. and M. Wallace, *Namibia, Women in War* (London: Zed, 1987).

Cohen, E. A., *Citizens and Soldiers: The Dilemmas of Military Service* (Ithaca and London: Cornell University Press, 1985).

Cornum, R., *She Went to War: The Rhonda Cornum Story* (Novato: Presidio Press, 1992).

Crolle, E., *Women's Rights in Government Policy in China since Mao* (London: Zed, 1983).

Deger, S. and T. Sen, *Military Expenditure: The Political Economy of International Security* (Stockholm: SIPRI, 1990).

Donne e guerra. Mito e storia (Udine: DARS, 1989).

Donne, guerra e società (Ancona: Il Lavoro Editoriale, 1982).

Dorn, E. (ed.) *Who Defends America? Race, Sex and Class in the Armed Forces* (Washington DC: Joint Committee for Political and Economic Studies, 1989).

Dumas, L. (ed.) *The Political Economy of Arms Reduction* (Westview: Boulder, 1982).

DWF, special issue on 'Donne ritrovate', March 1989.

Edwards Wersch, M., *Military Brats* (New York, Harmony, 1991).

Elshtain Bethke, J., *Public Man, Private Woman* (Princeton University Press, 1981).

Elshtain Bethke, J., *Women and War* (New York: Basic, 1987).

Elshtain Bethke, J. and S. Tobias (eds) *Women, Militarism and War: Essays in History, Politics and Social Theory* (Savage: Rowman and Littlefield, 1990).

Emanzipation in Uniform? Eine Diskussionsgrundlage/ Zusammengestellt von der Frauenkommission der POCH Zürich (Zürich, POCH, 1981).

Enloe, C., *Ethnic Soldiers* (Athens: University of Georgia Press, 1980).

Enloe, C., *Does Khaki Become You?* (London and New York: Pandora/Harper Collins, 1988).

Enloe, C., *Women and Militarization* (London: Change, 1991).

Ensign, T., *Military Life, The Insider Life* (Prentice: Hall Press, 1990).

Fourtouni, E., *Greek Women of the Resistance* (New Haven: Thelphini, 1986).

Fraser, A., *Boadicea's Chariot: The Warrior Queen* (London: Weidenfeld and Nicolson, 1988).

Frauen in den Streitkräften. Auswahlbibliographie (Bonn: Deutsche Bundestag, Wissenschafliche Dienst, 1988).

Freedman, D. and J. Rhoads (eds) *The Forgotten Vets: Nurses in Vietnam* (Austin: Texas Monthly, 1987).

Fullinwider, R. (ed.) *Conscript and Volunteer: Military Requirements, Social Justice and the All-Volunteer Force* (Totowa: Rowman and Allanheld, 1983).

Gallie, W. B., *Philosophers of Peace and War* (Cambridge: Cambridge University Press, 1978).

Gilligan, C., *In a Different Voice* (Cambridge Mass.: Harvard University Press, 1982).

Gioseffi, D. (ed.) *Women on War: Essential Voices for the Nuclear Age* (New York: Simon and Schuster, 1988).

Gluck, S. B., *Rosie the Riveter Revisited: Women, the War and Social Change* (New York: Twayne, 1987).

Goldin, C., *Understanding the Gender Gap* (Oxford: Oxford University Press, 1990).

Goldman, N. (ed.) *Female Soldiers: Combatants or Noncombatants? Historical and Contemporary Perspectives* (Westport: Greenwood, 1982).

Goldman, N. (ed.) *Women in the United States Armed Forces* (Chicago: Inter-University Seminar on Armed Forces and Society, 1984).

Graeff-Wassink, M., *Les femmes en armes. Kadhafi féministe?* (Paris: Armand Colin, 1990).

Greenwald, J., H. Connolly and P. Bloch, *New York City Policewomen on Patrol* (New York: Police Foundation, 1974).

Griffin, S., *The First and the Last: A Woman Thinks about War* (New York: Harper and Row, 1987).

Hartley, K. and T. Sandler (eds) *The Economics of Defence Spending* (London: Routledge, 1990).

Hartman, S., *The Home Front and Beyond: American Women in the 1940s* (Boston: Twayne, 1982).

Hauser, W., *America'a Army in Crisis: A Study in Civil–Military Relations* (Baltimore: Johns Hopkins University Press, 1973).

Higonnet, M. R., J. Jenson, S. Michel and M. C. Weitz (eds) *Behind the Lines: Gender and the Two World Wars* (New Haven: Yale University Press, 1987).

Hirschfeld, M., *The Sexual History of the World War* (New York: Falstaff Press Inc., 1937).

Holm, J., *Women in the Military: An Unfinished Revolution* (Novato: Presidio, 1982).

Holmes, R., *Acts of War* (New York: Free Press, 1985).

Honey, M., *Creating Rosie the Riveter: Class, Gender and Propaganda during World War II* (Amherst: University of Massachusetts Press, 1984).

Howe, F. (ed.), special issue of *Women's Studies Quarterly* on 'Teaching About Peace, War and the Women in the Military', 12 (1984).

Hunter, E. and D. Nice (eds.) *Military Families: Adaptation to Changes* (New York: Praeger, 1978).

Huntington, S., *The Soldier and the State: The Theory and Politics of Civil-Military Relations* (Cambridge: Belknap, 1957).

Huston, N. and S. Kinser, *A l'amour comme à la guerre* (Paris: Seuil, 1984).

Ilari, V., *Storia del servizio militare in Italia* (Rome: Riv. Militare, 1992).

Iqbal, S., *Woman and Islamic Law* (Lahore: Islamic Publications, n. d.).

Janssen, R., *Frauen ans Gewehr?* (Cologne: Pahl-Rugenstein, 1980).

Janovitz, M., *The Professional Soldier: A Social and Political Portrait* (Glencoe: Free Press, 1960).

Janovitz, M., *Military Conflict* (Beverly Hills: Sage, 1975).

Ilari V., *Storia del servizio militare in Italia* (Rome: Rivista Militare, 1992).

International Institute for Strategic Studies, *The Military Balance* (London: 1990).

Isaksson E. (ed.) *Women and the Military System* (London: Wheatsheaf, 1988).

Kamester, M. and J. Vellacott (eds) *Militarism versus Feminism: Writings on Women and War* (London: Virago, 1987).

Kann, M. E., *On the Man Question: Gender and Civic Virtue in America* (Philadelphia: Temple University Press, 1991).

Kanter, R., *Men and Women of the Corporation* (New York: Basic Books, 1977).

Kaslow, F. W., *The Military Family* (New York: Guilford Press, 1984).

Kleinbaum, A. W., *The War Against the Amazons* (New York: McGraw-Hill, 1983).

Laffin, J., *Women in Battle*, (New York/London: Abelard-Schuman, 1967).

Laska, V. (ed.) *Women in the Resistance and in the Holocaust: The Voices of Eyewitnesses* (Westport: Greenwood, 1983).

Lederar, W., *Gynecofobia ou la peur des femmes* (Paris: Payok, 1970).

Lippert, E. and T. Rössler, *Mädchen unter Waffen? Gesellschafts- und sozialpolitische Aspekte weiblicher Soldaten* (Baden-Baden: Nomos Verlag, 1980).

Loring, N. H. (ed.) *Women in the United States Armed Forces: Progress and Barriers in the 1980s* (Chicago: Inter-University Seminar on Armed Forces and Society, 1984).

McAllister, P., *Reweaving the Web of Life: Feminism and Nonviolence* (Philadelphia: New Society, 1982).

McCubbin, H., B. Dahal and E. Hunter (eds) *Families in the Military System* (Beverly Hills: Sage, 1976).

MacDonald, S., P. Holden and S. Ardener (eds) *Images of Women in Peace and War: Cross-Cultural and Historical Perspective* (London: Macmillan, and Madison: University of Wisconsin Press, 1987).

McGuigan D. G. (ed.), *The Role of Women in Conflict and Peace* (Ann Arbor: University of Michigan Press, 1977).

Mafai, M., *Pane nero. Donne e vita quotidiana nella seconda guerra mondiale* (Milan: Mondadori, 1987).

Mansfield, S., *The Gestalt of War: An Inquiry into the Origin and Meaning as a Social Institution* (New York: Dial Press, 1982).

Margiotta, F., J. Brown, M. J. Collins (eds) *Changing the US Military Manpower Realities* (Boulder: Westview, 1983).

Marshall, K., *In the Combat Zone* (New York: Penguin, 1987).

Martin, S. E., *Breaking and Entering* (Berkeley: University of California Press, 1980).

Marwick, A., *War and Social Change in the Twentieth Century* (London: Macmillan, 1974).

Marwick A. (ed) *Total War and Social Change in the twentieth Century* (New York: St Martin's Press, 1988).

Mead, M., *Male and Female* (New York: William Morrow, 1949).

Mead, M., *Sex and Temperament in Three Primitive Societies* (New York: William Morrow, 1963).

Menapace, L. and C. Ingrao (eds), *Né indifesa né in divisa* (Rome: Gruppo misto sinistra indipendente Regione Lazio, 1988).

Mernissi, F., *Sultanes oubliées. Femmes chefs d'Etat en Islam* (Paris: Albin Michel, 1990).

Mernissi, F., *Women and Islam: an Historical and Theological Enquiry* (Oxford: Basil Blackwell, 1991).

Milkman, R., *Gender at Work. The Dynamics of Job Segregation by Sex During World-War II* (Chicago: University of Illinois Press, 1987).

Moskos, C., *The American Enlisted Men: The Rank and File in Today's Military* (New York: Russell Sage Foundation, 1970).

Moskos, C. and R. F. Wood (eds), *The Military: More than a Job?* (Elmsford Park: Pergamon-Brassey's, 1988).

Muir, K., *Arms and the Woman* (London: Sinclair-Stevenson, 1992).

Mullaney, M. M., *Revolutionary Women* (New York: Praeger, 1983).

Nash, M., *Antifascist Resistance and Revolutionary Change: Women in the Spanish Civil War* (Denver: Arden Press, 1990).

NATO, *NATO Conference of Senior Service Women Officers of the Alliance, November 11–14, 1973* (Bruxelles: 1974).

NATO, *NATO Conference of Senior Service Women Officers of the Alliance, May 8–11, 1979* (The Hague: 1979).

NATO, *Women in the NATO Forces* (Brussels: 1986).

NATO, *Women in NATO: 30 Years of Progress and Success* (Brussels: 1991).

Partlow, F. A., *Womanpower for a Superpower: The National Security Implications of Women in the US Army* (Cambridge, Mass.: Center for International Affairs, 1983).

Pasquino, G., *Elementi per un controllo politico sulle forze armate* (Bologna: Il Mulino, 1975).

Perren, C., *Frauen und Militär sekretariat des Schweizerischen Friedensrates* (Zürich: 1979).

Pierson, R. R., *They're Still Women After All: The Second World War and Canadian Womanhood* (Toronto: McClelland and Stewart, 1986).

Pierson, R. R. (ed.) *Women and Peace: Theoretical, Historical and Practical Perspectives* (London: Croom Helm, 1987).

Portnay, D., *Women: The Recruiter's Last Resort* (Philadelphia: RECON, 1974).

Reardon, B., *Sexism and the War System* (New York: Teachers College Press, 1985).

Reeves, M., *Female Warriors of Allah: Women and the Islamic Revolution* (New York: Dutton, 1989).

Renov, M., *Hollywood's Wartime Woman: Representation and Ideology* (Ann Arbor: University Microfilms Inc., 1988).

Reti, special issue, *Le guerre che ho vissuto...*, January–April (1991).

Reynaud, E., *Les femmes, la violence et l'armée. Essai sur la féminisation des armées* (Paris: Fondation pour les études de defense nationale, 1988).

Ridd, R., and H. Callaway (eds) *Caught up in Conflict* (Basingstoke: Macmillan Education in association with the Oxford University Women's Studies Committee, 1986).

Rogan, H., *Mixed Company: Women in the Modern Army* (New York: Putnam, 1981).

Rothery, G. C., *The Amazons in Antiquity and Modern Times* (London: F. Griffiths, 1910).

Rupp, L. J., *Mobilizing Women for War: German American Propaganda 1939–1945* (Princeton University Press, 1978).

Rustad, M., *Women in Khaki: The American Enlisted Women* (New York: Praeger, 1982).

Samuel, P., *Amazones, guerrières et gaillardes* (Brussels: Edition Complexe, 1975).

Sanday, P., *Female Power and Male Dominance* (Cambridge University Press, 1981).

Sasson, J. P., *Princess* (New York: Doubleday, 1992).

Saywell, S., *Women in War* (New York: Viking, 1985).

Schecter, S., *Women and Male Violence* (Boston: South End Press, 1982).

Schmidt, C. and F. Blackaby (eds) *Peace, Defence and Economic Analysis* (London: Macmillan, 1987).

Schmitt, C., *Theorie des Partisanen: Zwischenbemerkung zum Begiff des Politischen* (Berlin: Duncker & Humblot, 1975).

Schmitt, C., *The Concept of Political* (Rutgers: Rutgers University Press, 1976).

Schneider, D., and C. Schneider, *Soundoff! American Military Women Speak Out* (New York: Dutton, 1988).

Segal, D., *Recruiting for Uncle Sam: Citizenship and Military Power Policy* (Lawrence: University Press of Kansas, 1989).

Segal, D. and J. Blair (eds) *Young Women in the Military*, special issue of *Youth and Society*, December 1978.

Segal, D. and W. Sinaiko, *Life in the Rank and File: Enlisted Men and Women in the Armed Forces of USA, Australia, Canada and the United Kingdom* (Washington: Pergamon-Brasseys International Defense Publishers, 1985).

Seidler, F., *Frauen zu den Waffen? Marketenderinnen, Helferinnen, Soldatinnen* (Koblenz/Bonn: Wehr und Wissen, 1978).

Il servizio militare femminile (Rome: Documentazione per le commissioni parlamentari, Camera dei Deputati, 1987).

Shepherd, S., *Amazons and Warrior Women: Varieties of Feminism in Seventeenth Century Drama* (New York: St. Martin's Press, 1981).

Sheriff, S., *Rights of Women in Islam* (London: Ta Ha, 1989).

Simmons, J., *Moral Principles and Political Obligations* (Princeton University Press, 1979).

Smith, H. L. (ed.) *War and Social Change: British Society in the Second World War* (Manchester University Press, 1986).

Steiner, G., *Antigones* (Oxford: Oxford University Press, 1986).

Stiehm, J. H., *Bring Me Men and Women: Mandated Change at the US Air Force Academy* (Berkeley: University of California Press, 1981).

Stiehm, J. and M. Saint-Germain, *Men, Women and State Violence: Government and the Military* (Washington: American Political Science Association, 1983).

Stiehm, J. H., *Arms and the Enlisted Woman* (Philadelpia: Temple University Press, 1989).

Stiehm J. H., (ed.) *Women and Men's Wars*, special issue of *Women's Studies International Forum*, 3–4 (1982).

Stiehm J. H. (ed.) *Women's View of the Political World of Men* (New York: Transnational Publishers, 1984).

Stricker, W., *Die Amazonen in Sage und Geschichte* (Berlin: Sammlung Gemeinverständlicher Wissenschaflicher Vorträge, 1868).

Summerfield, P., *Women Workers in the Second World War: Production and Patriarchy in Conflict* (London: Croom Helm, 1984).

Sweezy, P., *Monopoly Capital* (Harmondsworth: Penguin, 1975, 1st edition, 1966).

Tannen, D., *You Just Don't Understand* (New York: Ballantine, 1990).

Taylor, P. M., *War and the Media: Propaganda and Persuasion in the Gulf War* (Manchester University Press, 1992).

Thomas, J. and D. Prather, *Integration of Females to Previous All-Male Institution*, Proceedings of the Fifth Symposium on Psychology in the Air Force (Colorado Springs: April 1976).

Thomson, D. (ed.) *Over Our Dead Bodies: Women Against the Bomb* (London: Virago, 1983).

Tiger, L., *Men in Groups* (New York: Random House, 1969).

Tilly, C., *Coercion, Capital and European States, AD 990–1990* (Cambridge: Basil Blackwell, 1990).

Tobias, S., and L. Anderson, *What Really Happened to Rosie the Riveter: Demobilization and the Female Labor Force* (New York: 1974).

Treadwell, M., *United States Army in World War II: Special Studies – The Women's Army Corps* (Washington: Office of Chief of Military History, Department of the Army, 1954).

Tyrell, W. B., *Amazons: A Study in Athenian Mythmaking* (Baltimore: Johns Hopkins University Press, 1984).

van Devanter, L., *Home Before Morning* (New York: Beaufort, 1983).

Wadge D. C., (ed.) *Women in Uniform* (London: Sampson Low Marston, 1946).

Waite. L. J., and S. E. Berryman, *Women in Nontraditional Occupations: Choice and Turnover* (Santa Monica: Rand, 1985).

Walker, K., *A Piece of My Heart* (New York: Ballantine, 1985).

Warner, M., *Joan of Arc: The Image of Female Heroism* (New York: Vintage, 1982).

Wertsch, M., *Military Brats: The Legacy of Childwood Inside the Fortress* (New York: Crown, 1991).

Wheelwright, J., *Amazons and Military Maids: Women Who Dressed as Men in the Pursuit of Life, Liberty and Happiness* (London: Pandora, 1989).

Wilder, A., *Man and Women, War and Peace: The Strategists' Companion* (London and New York, Routledge and Kegan Paul, 1987).

Willenz, J. A., *Women Veterans: America's Forgotten Heroines* (New York: Continuum Press, 1983).

Williams, C., *Gender Differences at Work: Women and Men in Nontraditional Occupations* (Berkeley: University of California Press, 1989).

Wiltsher, A., *Most Dangerous Women: Feminist Peace Campaigners of the Great War* (London: Pandora, 1985).

Windrow M., (ed.) *Women at War, 1939–1945* London: Osprey,1980.

Wolf, C., *Cassandra: A Novel and Four Essays* (New York: Farrar, Straus & Giroux, 1981).

Women and the Gulf War (New York: Church Women United, 1991).

Women in the Military, Hearings before the Military Personnel and Compensation Subcommittee of the Committee on Armed Services of the House of Representatives (Washington: US Government Printing Office, 1990).

Woolf, V., *Three Guineas* (New York: Harcourt Brace, 1938).

Zafrulla Khan, M., *A Clarification of the Myth in the West about the Status of a Woman in Islam* (Tilford: Islam International Publications, 1988).

ARTICLES IN BOOKS AND JOURNALS

Abed, A. J., 'An Army Career: 1945–1968: An Interview with Major Edith N. Straw, USA (Ret.)', *Minerva* (1985) pp. 95–126.

Adams, J., 'Attitudinal Studies on the Integration of Women at West Point', *International Journal of Women's Studies*, 1 (1982) pp. 22–8.

Adams, J., 'Women at West Point: A Three Year Perspective', *Sex Roles*, 11 (1984) pp. 525–41.

Addis, E. and N. Tiliacos, 'Conflict, Fear and Security in the Nuclear Age: The Challange of the Feminist Peace Movement in Italy', *Radical America*, 20 (1986) pp. 7–15.

Adolf, H., 'Literary Characters and their Subterranean Sources: The Amazon Type in Literature', in *Proceedings of the 2nd Congress of the International Comparative Literature Association* (Chapel Hill: The Orange Printshop, 1959) pp. 256–63.

Allen, M., 'The Domestic Ideal and the Mobilization of Womenpower in World War II', *Women's Studies*, 4 (1983) pp. 401–412.

Alvagnini, D., 'Donne e stellette. Panorama sul servizio militare femminile', *Rivista aeronautica*, May–June (1990), pp. 18–25 (1st part).

Angrist, J. D., 'The Effects of Veteran Benefits on Veteran's Education and Earnings', *NBER Working Papers*, 3492 (1990).

Angrist J. D. and A. Krueger, 'Why do World War II Veterans Earn more than Nonveterans?', *NBER Working Papers*, 2991 (1989).

Angrist, S. S., 'The Study of Sex Roles', *Journal of Social Issues,* 25 (1969) pp. 215–32.

Arkin, W. and L. Dobrofsky, 'Military Socialization and Masculinity', *Journal of Social Issues,* 34 (1978) pp. 151–68.

Attebury, M. A., 'Women and their Wartime Roles', *Minerva* (1990) pp. 11–28.

Bacevich, A. J., 'Family Matters: American Civilian and Military Elites in the Progressive Era', *Armed Forced and Society,* 3 (1982) pp. 405–18.

Bayes, M. and P. M. Newton, 'Women in Authority: A Sociopsychological Analysis', *Journal of Applied Behavioral Science,* 14 (1978) pp. 7–20.

Beauchamp, V. W., 'The Sisters and the Soldiers', *Maryland Historical Magazine* (1986) pp. 117–33.

Bearayt, C., 'Women in the US Armed Services: The War in the Persian Gulf', Women's Research and Education Institute, 1700 13th St, NW, Suite 400, Wasington DC, 1991.

Bérubé, A. and J. D'Emilio, 'The Military and Lesbians during the McCarthy Years', *Signs* (1984) pp. 759–75.

Bloch, R. H., 'The Gendered Meanings of Virtue in Revolutionary America', *Signs* (1987) pp. 37–58.

Bonetti, P. 'Il dibattito sulla condizione militare in un anno difficile', *II Mulino,* 1 (1987) pp. 116–29.

Brandt, G. C., '"Pigeon-Holed and Forgotten": the Work of the Subcommittee on the Post-War Problems of Women, 1943', *Histoire sociale/Social History,* May (1982) pp. 239–59.

Bravo, A., 'Introduzione' in A. Bravo (ed.), *Donne e uomini nelle guerre mondiali* (Rome–Bari: Laterza,1991)

Brotz, H. and E. Wilson, 'Characteristics of Military Society', *American Journal of Sociology,* 51 (1946) pp. 371–5.

Brown, S. A., 'Recovering the History of Western Military Women', *Minerva* (1984) pp. 83–97.

Campbell, D'A., 'Servicewomen of World War II', *Armed Forces and Society,* 2 (1990) pp. 251–70.

Cappuzzo, U., 'Tra focolare e campo di Marte', *Rivista Militare,* 6 (1982) pp. 2–8.

Cheatham, H., 'Attitudes Toward Women in the Military: Implications for Counselors', in *Proceedings of the Second Service Academy Counseling Conference* (New London, 1978).

Cheatham, H., 'Integration of Women into the US Military', *Sex Roles,* 1 (1984) pp. 141–51.

Clark, A. P., 'Women at the Service Academies and Combat Leadership', *Strategic Review,* 5 (1977).

Cooper, S., 'The Work of Women in Nineteenth Century Continental European Peace Movements', *Peace and Change* (1984) pp. 11–28.

Cottam, K. J., 'Soviet Women in Combat in World War II: The Ground Forces and the Navy', *International Journal of Women's Studies,* July–August (1980) pp. 345–57.

Cottam, K. J., 'Soviet Women in Combat in World War II: The Rear Services, Resistance behind Enemy Lines and Political Workers', *International Journal of Women's Studies,* September–October (1982) pp. 363–78.

Curti, M., 'Reflections on the Genesis and Growth of Peace History', *Peace and Change*, Spring (1985) pp. 1–18.

Deaux K., and T. Emswiller, 'Explanation of Successful Performance on Sex-linked Tasks: What's Skill for the Male is Luck for the Female', *Journal of Personality and Social Psychology*, 29 (1974) pp. 80–5.

De Fleur, L. B., 'Organizational and Ideological Barriers to Sex Integration in Military Groups', *Work and Occupation*, 12 (1985) pp. 206–28.

De Fleur, L. B. and D. Gillman, 'Cadet Beliefs, Attitudes and Interactions during the Early Phases of Sex Integration', *Youth and Society*, 10 (1978) pp. 389–90.

De Fleur, L. B. and R. L. Warner, 'Air Force Academy Graduates and Nongraduates: Attitudes and Self-Concepts', *Armed Forces and Society*, 4 (1987) pp. 517–33.

De Grazia, S., 'Political Equality and Military Participation', *Armed Forces and Society*, 11 (1985) pp. 181–6.

Dekker, R. M. and L. C. van de Pol, 'Republican Heroines: Cross-Dressing Women in the French Revolutionary Armies', *History of European Ideas*, 3 (1989) pp. 353–64.

Dengler, B., 'Acceptance and Avoidance: The Woman Vietnam Vet', *Minerva* (1987) pp. 72–96.

Devilbiss, M. C., 'Gender Integration and Unit Deployment: A Study of GI Jo', *Armed Forces and Society*, 4 (1985) pp. 523–52.

De Waal, F., 'Sex Differences in the Stability of Friendship and Rivalries among Chimpanzees', Paper presented at the 10th Conference of the ISRA (International Society for Research on Aggression) Siena, 6–12 November 1992.

Di Stefano, G., 'L'accesso delle donne alla carriera militare' *Rivista militare*, 4 (1990) pp. 44–54.

Dobrofsky, L., 'Women's Power and Authority in the Context of War', *Sex Roles*, 2 (1977) pp. 141–57.

Dobrofsky, L., 'Military Socialization and Masculinity', *Journal of Social Issues*, 34 (1978) pp. 151–68.

Downes, C. J., 'To Be or Not to Be a Profession: The Military Case', *Defense Analysis*, 3 (1985) pp. 147–71.

Duke, D. C., 'Spy Scares, Scapegoats, and the Cold War', *South Atlantic Quarterly* (1980) pp. 245–78.

Dunvin, K., 'Gender and Perceptions of the Job Environment in the US Air Force', *Armed Forces and Society*, 1 (1988) pp. 71–91.

Durning, K. P., 'Attitudes of Enlisted Women and Men Toward the Navy', *Armed Forces and Society*, 1 (1982) pp. 20–32.

Emo, D. M., S. Hall and D. Kern, '1964: Vietnam and the Army Nursing', *Minerva* (1990) pp. 49–67.

Enloe, C., 'Women. The Reserve Army of Army Labour', *Review of Radical Political Economics*, 2 (1980) pp. 42–52.

Enloe, C., 'Feminist Thinking about War, Militarism, and Peace', in B. B. Hess and M. M. Ferree, *Analyzing Gender: A Handbook of Social Science Research* (Beverly Hills: Sage, 1987) pp. 526–47.

Enloe, C., 'The Gendered Gulf', in C. Peters (ed.) *Collateral Damage* (Boston: South End Press, 1991).

Enloe, C., and H. Jordan, 'Black Women in the Military', *Minerva* (1985) pp. 108–16.

Elshtain Bethke, J., 'Women as Mirror and Others: Toward a Theory of Women, War, and Feminism', *Humanities in Society* (1982).

Fainsod Katzenstein, M., 'Feminism Within American Institutions: Unobtrusive Mobilization in the 1980s', *Signs*, 16 (1990) 2, pp. 27–54.

Faqir, F., 'Beyond the Desert Storm', *Planet* (1985).

Faqir, F., 'Tales of War: Arab Women in the Eye of the Storm', in *The Gulf Between Us* (London: Virago Press, 1991) pp. 77–88.

Ferrarotti, F., 'Introduction' to F. Ferrarotti (ed.) *Comte. Antologia di scritti sociologici* (Bologna: Il Mulino, 1977).

Fraddosio, M., 'La donna e la guerra. Aspetti della militanza femminile nel fascismo dalla mobilitazione civile alle origini del SAF nella Repubblica Sociale italiana', *Storia Contemporanea*, December (1989) pp. 1105–81.

Fuentes, A., 'Equality, Yes – Militarism, No', *The Nation*, 28 October 1991.

Gilbert, S., 'Soldier's Heart: Literary Men, Literary Women, and the Great War', *Signs*, 8 (1983) pp. 422–50.

Goldman, N., 'The Utilization of Women in the Armed Forces of NATO Countries', *Military Review*, October (1974) pp. 72–82.

Goldman, N., 'The Utilization of Women in the Armed Forces of Industrialized Nations', *Sociological Symposium* (1977) pp. 1–23.

Goldman, N., 'The Changing Role of Women in the Armed Forces', *American Journal of Sociology*, 4 (1978) pp. 892–911.

Goodson, S. H., 'Capt. Joy Bright Hancock and the Role of Women in the US Navy', *New Jersey History* (1987) pp. 1–18.

Gordon, L., 'The Peaceful Sex? On Feminism and the Peace Movement', *NWSA Journal* (1990) pp. 624–34.

Gravois, M., 'Military Families in Germany, 1946–1986: Why They Came and Why They Stay', *Parameters* (1986) pp. 57–67.

Gregory-Lewis, S., 'Lesbians in the Military', in *Our Right to Love: A Lesbian Resource Book* (Englewood: Prentice-Hall, 1978) pp. 211–16.

Griesse, A. E., M. A. Harlow, 'Soldiers of Happenstance: Women in Soviet Uniform', *Minerva* (1985) pp. 127–51.

Gundersen, J. R., 'Independence, Citizenship, and the American Revolution', *Signs* (1987) pp. 59–77.

Gunderson, M., 'Male–Female Wage Differentials and Policy Responses', *Journal of Economic Literature*, March (1989).

Hacker, B. C., 'Women and Military Institutions in Early Modern Europe: A Reconnaissance', *Signs* (1981) pp. 643–71.

Hacker, B. C., 'Where Have all the Women Gone? The Pre-Twentieth Century Sexual Division of Labour in Armies', *Minerva* (1985) pp. 107–48.

Hedin, B. A., 'Through a Glass Darkly: Vietnam, Alienation, and Passion', *Minerva* (1988) pp. 51–68.

Hietanen, A., 'Women in the Military System: Historical Myths and Contemporary Problems', in K. Kiljunen and J. Väänänen (eds.) *Youth and Conscription* (Helsinki: Peace Union of Finland, 1987) pp. 99–106.

Hobfoll S. E., and P. London, 'The Relationship of Self Concept and Social Support to Emotional Distress among Women during War', *Journal of Social and Clinical Psychology*, 40 (1986) pp. 189–203.

Hoffman, S., 'The Acceptability of Military Force', *Adelphi Paper*, 102, *Force in Modern Societies: Its Place in International Politics* (London: ISS, 1973), pp. 2–13.

Hoiberg, A., 'Military Psychology and Women's Role in the Military', in R. Gale and A. D. Mangelsdorff (eds) *Handbook of Military Psychology* (Chichester: John Wiley, 1991) pp. 725–39.

Hoiberg, A. and J. Ernst, 'Motherhood in the Military: Conflicting Roads for Navy Women', *International Journal of Sociology of the Family*, 10 (1980), pp. 265–80.

Hoiberg, A. and P. J. Thomas, 'The Economics of Sex Integration: An Update of Binkin and Bach', *Defense Management Journal*, 18 (1982), pp. 18–25.

Hoiberg, A. and J. F. White, 'Health Status of Women in the Armed Forces', *Armed Forces and Society*, 4 (1992) pp. 514–33.

Hooker, R. D., 'Affirmative Action and Combat Exclusion: Gender Roles in the US Army', *Parameters*, December (1989) pp. 36–50.

Howard, M., 'Temperamenta Belli: Can War be Controlled?', in M. Howard (ed.) *Restraints on War* (Oxford: Oxford University Press, 1979).

Huston, N., 'The Matrix of War: Mothers and Heroes', in S. R. Suleiman (ed.) *The Female, Body in Western Culture* (Cambridge, Mass.: Harvard University Press, 1985).

Izraeli, D., 'Sex Effects or Structural Effects?', *Social Forces*, 1 (1983) pp. 153–65.

Kanter, R. M., 'Some Effects of Proportions on Group Life: Skewed Sex-Ratios and Responses to Token Women', *American Journal of Sociology*, 82 (1977) pp. 965–90.

Kleinbaum, A. W., 'Amazon Dreams: Feminism and the Amazon Image', *Minerva* (1985) pp. 95–106.

Klick, J., 'Utilization of Women in the NATO Alliance', *Armed Forces and Society* (1978) pp. 673–678.

Kumka, D. S. and J. Silverman, 'Gender Differences in Attitudes towards Nuclear War and Disarmament', *Sex Roles*, 3–4 (1987) pp. 189–202.

Lamerson, C. D., 'The Evolution of a Mixed-Gender Canadian Forces', *Minerva* (1989) pp. 12–24.

Lawson, J. E., '"She's a Pretty Woman...for a Gook": the Misogyny of the Vietnam War', *Journal of American Culture* (1989) pp. 55–66.

Loraux, N., 'Le Lit, la Guerre', *L'Homme*, 21 (1981) pp. 37–67.

Manley, K. B., 'Women of Los Alamos during World War II: Some of Their Views', *New Mexico Historical Review*, April (1990) pp. 251–66.

Marin, S., 'Police Women and Policewomen: Occupational Role Dilammas and Choice of Female Officers', *Journal of Police Science and Administration*, 3 (1979) pp. 314–23.

Martin, M. L., 'From Periphery to Center: Women in the French Military', *Armed Forces and Society* (1982) pp. 303–33.

McKenney, J. E., '"Women in Combat": Comment', *Armed Forces and Society*, 4 (1982) pp. 686–92.

McLaughlin, M., 'The Woman Warrior: Gender, Warfare and Society in Medieval Europe', *Women's Studies*, 3–4 (1990) pp. 193–210.

Mincer, J., 'Intercountry Comparisons of Labour Force Trends and of Related Developments: An Overview', *Journal of Labour Economics*, January (1985).

Mini, F., 'Soldato "Joe" e soldato "Jane"', *Rivista Militare*, 3 (1983) pp. 37–49.

Modell J., and D. Steffey, 'Waging War and Marriage: Military Service and Family Formation, 1940–1950', *Journal of Family History*, 2 (1988) pp. 195–218.

Moore, B. L., 'Black, Female and in Uniform: An African-American Woman in the United States Army, 1973–1979', *Minerva* (1990) pp. 62–6.

Moreau, J., 'Les guerrières et les femmes impudiques', in *Mélanges Henri Grégoire, Annuaire de Philologie et d'Histoire Orientales et Slaves* (Brussels, 1951).

Moskos, C., 'From Institution to Occupation: Trends in Military Organization', *Armed Forces and Society*, 1 (1977) pp. 41–50.

Moskos, C., 'Female GIs in the Field', *Society*, 22 (1985) pp. 28–33.

Moskos, C., 'Institutional/Occupational: Trends in Armed Forces – An Update', *Armed Forces and Society*, 3 (1986) pp. 377–82.

Nabors, R., 'Women in the Army: Do They Measure Up?', *Military Review*, 10 (1982) pp. 51–61.

Nash, M., 'Militianas and Homefront Heroines: Images of Women in Revolutionary Spain', *History of European Ideas*, 11 (1989) pp. 235–244.

Nocilla, D., 'Servizio militare femminile e Costituzione', *Diritto e societa*', 1 (1981) pp. 161–80.

Ott, E. M., 'The Impact of the Admission of Women to the Service Academies on the Role of the Woman Line Officer', *American Behavioral Scientist*, 19 (1976) pp. 647–64.

Pedersen, S., 'Gender, Welfare, and Citizenship in Britain during the Great War', *American Historical Review*, October (1990) pp. 983–1006.

Priest, R., 'Evolutionary versus Revolutionary Changes in Military Academy Cadets', in F. Margiotta (ed.), *Changing World of the American Military* (Boulder: Westview, 1978), pp. 367–81.

Priest, R., H. Prince and A. Vitters, 'The First Coed Class at West Point', *Youth and Society*, 2 (1978) pp. 205–224.

Quester, G., 'Women in Combat', *International Security* (1977) pp. 80–91.

Roden, D., 'From Old Miss to New Professional: A Portrait of Women Educators under the American Occupation of Japan, 1945–1952', *History of Education Quarterly* (1983) pp. 469–89.

Rosen, S. and P. Taubman, 'Changes in Life Cycle Earnings: What do Social Security Data Show?', *Journal of Human Resources*, 17 (1982) pp. 321–38.

Rottman, M., 'Women Graduates of the US Coast Guard Academy: Views from the Bridges', *Armed Forces and Society*, 2 (1985) pp. 249–70.

Sassor J. P., *Princess* (New York: Doubleday, 1992)

Scott, J.,'Gender: A Useful Category of Historical Analysis', *American Historical Review*, 91 (1986).

Saxonhouse, A., 'Men, Women, War and Politics: Family and Polis in Aristophanes and Euripides', *Political Theory*, 8 (1980) pp. 65–81.

Saulle, M. R. 'Il servizio militare femminile e le convenzioni internazionali', *Rivista militare*, 3 (1981) pp. 89–93.

Segal, D. R., N. S. Kinzer and J. C. Woelfel, 'The Concept of Citizenship and Attitutes toward Women in Combat', *Sex Roles*, 5 (1977) pp. 469–77.

Segal, D. R., J. G. Bachman and F. Dowdell, 'Military Service for Female and Black Youth: A Perceived Mobility Opportunity', *Youth and Society*, 10, December (1978) pp. 191–204.

Segal, M. W., 'The Military and the Family as Greedy Institutions', *Armed Forces and Society*, 1 (1986) pp. 9–38.

Segal, M. W., 'Women in the Military: Research and Policy Issues', *Youth and Society*, 10 (1978) pp. 101–26.

Segal, M. W., and D. R. Segal, 'Social Change and Participation of Women in the American Military', in L. Kriesberg (ed.) *Research in Social Movements, Conflicts and Change*, 5 (Greenwich: JAI Press, 1983) pp. 235–58.

'Il servizio militare femminile in Francia', *Rivista Militare*, May–June (1990) pp. 101–7.

'Il servizio militare femminile', *Annuario ISTRID* (1980–81) pp. 485–99.

Shermann, J., '"They Either Need these Women or They Do Not": Margaret Chase Smith and the Fight for Regular Status for Women in the Military', *Journal of Military History*, January (1990) pp. 47–78.

Sowerwine, C., 'Women against the War: a Feminine Basis for Internationalism and Pacifism?', *Western Society for French History*, November (1978) pp. 361–70.

Spangler, E., M. Gordon and R. Pipkin, 'Token Women: An Empirical Test of Kanter's Hypothesis', *American Journal of Sociology*, 1 (1978) pp. 160–70.

Spelts, D., 'The Women Who Died in Vietnam', *Minerva* (1985) pp. 89–96.

Stanley, S. C. and M. W. Segal, 'Military Women in NATO: An Update', *Armed Forces and Society*, 4 (1988) pp. 559–85.

Stiehm, J. H., 'The Generations of US Enlisted Women', *Signs*, 1 (1985) pp. 155–75.

Taricone, F., 'Le donne soldato', *Rivista Militare*, 1 (1985) pp. 108–16.

Tricarico, A., 'Le donne nelle forze armate: un'indagine tra gli allievi dell'Accademia', *Rivista Aeronautica*, 5 (1982) pp. 22–7.

Tuten, J. M., 'Women in Military Service', *Armed Forces and Society* (1981) pp. 160–3.

Willard, C. C., 'Early Images of Female Warrior: Minerva, the Amazons, Joan of Arc', *Minerva* (1988) pp. 1–11.

Willenz, J. A., 'Women Veterans from the Vietnam War Through the Eighties', *Minerva* (1988) pp. 61–6.

Wright, A., 'The Role of US Army Women in Grenada', *Minerva*, 2 (1984) pp. 103–13.

Yoder, J. D., J. Adams and H. T. Prince, 'The Price of a Token', *Journal of Political and Military Sociology*, 11 (1985) pp. 323–37.

Yuval-Davis, N., 'Front and Rear: The Sexual Division of Labor in the Israeli Army', *Feminist Studies*, 3 (1985) pp. 649–75.

Zemon Davis, N., 'Women's History in Transition: the European Case', *Feminist Studies*, 3 (1975–6) p. 90.

Zemon Davis, N., 'Men, Women and Violence: Some Reflections on Equality', *Smith Alumnae Quarterly*, April (1977) pp. 12–15.

Zur O., and A. Morrison, 'Gender and War: Reexamining Attitudes', *American Journal of Orthopsychiatry*, 4 (1989) pp. 528–33.

Index